REMEMBERING
THE DAYS OF SORROW

REMEMBERING THE DAYS OF SORROW

The WPA and the Texas Slave Narratives

Ronald E. Goodwin

State House Press
Buffalo Gap, Texas

Library of Congress Cataloging-in-Publication Data

Goodwin, Ronald E.
Remembering the Days of Sorrow: The WPA and the Texas Slave Narratives
Ronald E. Goodwin
    p. cm.
Includes Bibliographical references and index.
ISBN- 978-1-933337-47-0(pbk. alk. paper)
ISBN- 933337-47-8 (pbk. alk. paper)
1. History United States 2. History / African American Studies 3. United States: History-19th century. 4. Texas History / African American Studies, Texas
This paper meets the requirements of ANSI/NISO, Z39.48-1992 (permanence of paper) Binding materials have been chosen for durability ♽ ∞
I. Title.
    "Cataloging-in-Publication Data available from the Library of Congress"

Manufactured in the United States
Copyright 2013, State House Press
All Rights Reserved
First Edition

State House Press
P.O. Box 818
Buffalo Gap, Texas 79508
325-572-3974 · 325-572-3991 (fax)
www.tfhcc.com

No part of this book may be reproduced in any form unless with written permission from State House Press, except for brief passages by reviewers.

Printed in the United States of America
Distributed by Texas A&M University Press Consortium
800-826-8911
www.tamupress.com

ISBN-13: 978-1-933337-47-0
ISBN-10: 1-933337-47-8

Book Design by Rosenbohm Graphic Design

Therefore, my beloved brethren, be steadfast, immovable, always abounding in the work of the Lord, knowing that your toil is not in vain in the Lord.
1 Corinthians 15:58

Let us not lose heart in doing good, for in due time we will reap if we do not grow weary.
Galatians 6:9

CONTENTS

Preface		ix
Acknowledgments		xiii
Part One	**The Government, the New Deal, and Aging Ex-Slaves**	1
One	The WPA and the Slave Narratives	3
Two	Remembering Slavery in Texas	13
Part Two	**Masters and Slaves**	23
Three	The Master	25
Four	The Plantation's Labor	37
Five	Fight the Power	49
Six	The Slave Family	61
Seven	The Conditions of Slavery	77
Part Three	**Freedom and the War of the Lost Cause**	95
Eight	The War and Emancipation	97
Nine	Life after Slavery	111
Ten	Changing Slavery's Paradigm	129
Notes		139
Bibliography		165
Index		171

PREFACE

During the Great Depression, ninety-year-old Ben Simpson answered questions about his life as a slave. He shared with his Works Progress Administration (WPA) interviewer that both his parents were captured in Africa and brought to Georgia, his birthplace, as slaves. Simpson described his owner as a "killer" who eventually left Georgia and forced his slaves to walk to Texas. Simpson did not mention how old he was when his family left Georgia, but he remembered that his mother died on that treacherous journey.

> Massa have a great, long whip platted out of rawhide and when on[e] the niggers fall behind or give out, he hit him with that whip. It take the hide every time he hit a nigger. Mother, she gave out on the way, 'bout the line of Texas. Her feet got raw and bleedin' and her legs swoll plumb out of shape. Then massa, he jus' take out he gun and shot her, and whilst she lay dyin' he kicks her two, three times and say, 'Damn a nigger what can't stand nothin'.'

Although it may seem unreasonable to comment on another person's life as "typical," Simpson's experiences during slavery were just that. As a child he saw his mother killed, he slept on the ground, and had little food to eat. He even remembered his only sister being sold soon after giving birth to a child. She was only fifteen and the master's "wife" until he got married. One wonders what effects these experiences might have had on a young child. Throughout all of the pain experienced in his life, Simpson was ready to see God, but there was one condition. "I's ready to see God but I hope my old massa ain't there to torment me again." Almost seventy years after the end of slavery, Simpson never forgot the image of his mother dying on the road and his vicious killer–owner stomping and cursing her as if she was not dying fast enough. Simpson never could erase those images from his mind.

Like many blacks born during the civil rights movement of the 1960s, I was blessed with a family that believed in the omnipotence of the almighty God. My great-grandfather, the Reverend Shelly Edward Steward, or Big Pappa, as black Southerners often referred to their grandfathers, was the pastor and founder of the Shiloh Missionary Baptist Church in San Antonio, Texas. His spiritual and moral influences still resonate in my life. However, as a child I did not always embrace these influences. I remember vividly that as teenager I often ran from Big Pappa as he entered the sanctuary on Sundays. But every Sunday, without fail, he would find me. It was not that I did not want to speak to him; it was that he always said the same things to me. Even when his eyesight was failing, he would recognize my voice, smile, and say, "You're one of Betty's boys." I would reply, "Yes sir." And then he would proceed with what I considered his familiar rhetoric. "You will be measured from your neck up. It does not matter how fast you can run, or how far you can kick or throw a ball, you will always be measured from your neck up."

Even now, years later, I cringe as I admit that I did not understand what this meant. After all, I already had my life planned out. I'd go to a major college, be a football star, move on to the National Football League, have my jersey retired at the end of an all-pro career, and make commercials, in which I'd either endorse beer or soda, throw my jersey to some wide-eyed kid, or run through airports hurdling turnstiles with ease. Needless to say, none of that happened for me, just like it did not happen for thousands of black kids growing up in the 1960s and 1970s.

But what did, "you will be measured from your neck up" mean? It was not until I joined the military—after my first foray into academics ended miserably—that I finally understood what he meant. I found myself assigned to dig a garden on a military base in San Antonio in the middle of a January heat spell. As I pushed that shovel, otherwise known as an "idiot stick," into the dirt, I wondered what planting flowers had to do with defending my country and national defense. "So this is it." I thought to myself. "Without an education this is my future: digging in the dirt. So this is what it must have felt to be a slave!" At that moment, I experienced my first real epiphany! "Now," I smiled to myself, "I understand what Big Pappa was saying. His generation, and those before him, struggled in the fields working endless hours on someone else's land, and then suffered through the indignities of Jim Crow racism so I would not have to." Granted, by the 1970s, the racial barriers that limited blacks were *mostly* gone. There were still remnants of racism, as today, but by and large, blacks could go to any school and pursue any career they wanted, even that of being a football star.

But by the time of this initial awakening, I am ashamed to admit that I had not paid enough reverence to those who came before me. I read about such notable blacks as Malcolm X, Martin Luther King, Jr., W. E. B. DuBois, Booker T. Washington, and Marcus Garvey, usually during the month of February. And I was, for a time, a little radical like the television character Michael Evans, the "militant midget," from the 1970s black sitcom *Good Times*. Still, I did not fully understand the struggles of people like Medgar Evers and Frederick Douglass, or why someone would want to kill Emmitt Till, a black teenager visiting relatives in the South one summer vacation. "I'm going to be a football star," I kept telling myself, "why do I need to focus on all that old stuff?" Why indeed!

With the dawn of a new century, there is a new generation of black children also dreaming of glory on football fields or basketball courts. Even my own sons have dreams of going from high school to the NBA à la Kobe Bryant and LeBron James. After watching the NBA finals one year, and listening to their aspirations of being an eighteen-year-old phenom in the NBA, I impatiently interjected, "Stop dreaming about basketball. I doubt that you will grow to be 6'8." You will be known from your neck up." So there it was; the circle of life was now complete! I found myself in the position of having to educate my sons about the struggles of those blacks who gave up their comfort, and oftentimes their lives, so they could have the opportunities Big Pappa only dreamt of.

In 1959, historian Stanley Elkins wrote about the similarities of black slavery and the German concentration camps during the Second World War. He argued that those subjected to some form of authoritarian rule usually behave in the same manner. For example, some will begin to identify with their oppressors, whereas others will assume an infantile-like demeanor and attitude in which they act helpless and dependent on their oppressors. In fact, Elkins introduced his now-famous *Sambo* caricature, which he used to describe the behavior of black slaves in the antebellum South as being lazy and childlike, in particular black male slaves. Scores of historians have successfully challenged the Sambo caricature over the last thirty years, illustrating that blacks were not as docile as Elkins believed.

Preface

This book is not merely another attempt to revise this misrepresentation of the attitudes and behaviors of the former slaves during slavery. Instead, this book uses the oral narratives of the Texas Slaves' Narratives Project, which was a WPA program designed to support the social and economic agenda of President Franklin D. Roosevelt's New Deal, to give hundreds of surviving ex-slaves the opportunity to tell *their* stories of slavery. Many of the ex-slaves were feeble and frail, and some eagerly anticipated death. Some willingly told their stories, whereas others hesitatingly agreed.

Nonetheless, this was their opportunity to tell a new generation of blacks, and whites, how barbaric it was to be a slave owned by another human being. They talked about their former masters, overseers, marriages, religion, and other aspects of their antebellum lives, while fighting to maintain their dignity in the face of unspeakable horrors.

These individuals are our great-great-great grandparents, aunts, uncles, and cousins, and their voices resonate through time and show us a world some—black and white—would like to forget. Their voices are as important today as they were in the 1930s because many do not know how blacks lived, nor do they know how blacks survived slavery *or* the Great Depression. As a result, these oral narratives provide glimpses into black life and culture during two of the most distressing times in US history: slavery and the Great Depression, when to be black meant being confined to the lower rungs of US society.

Further, because the WPA national and state administrators hoped that there would be some consistency between interviews, the administrators instructed the interviewers to adhere as closely as possible to the approved questions. These questions, which may seem elementary on some levels, provide a foundation for the slaves to tell about their every day life, and some, along with their answers, can be found in the part openers throughout the book.

This book also illustrates to a new generation that blacks have not always lived in homes with three bedrooms and two-and-a-half baths. Blacks have not always been able to attend their state's flagship universities or marry anyone they fell in love with. There are too many aspects of the present black community that are taken for granted. It is my desire to remind everyone, old and young alike, of the struggles and hardships endured by our ancestors in Texas and this country, so that we will never forget.

ACKNOWLEDGMENTS

This story is a personal one for me. Like many good stories, it has had its own twists and turns and ups and downs. Throughout the research for this story there were some days when I could not contain my excitement, and then there were those days when I literally did not feel that I could go on. It was in those "dark" days that I came to value those individuals who encouraged and supported not only this research but also me as a person.

I'd like to thank the following people for setting me on this path of discovery (personal and professional). Naomi Ledé and Carol A. Lewis encouraged me to always be professional, to have character, and display the kind of dignity befitting the descendants of those who survived slavery and Jim Crow segregation. Cary Wintz believed enough in my academic potential that he persuaded me to reach higher than I ever thought possible. I thank John Moretta for putting his own reputation on the line in support of me. He will never know the depths of my appreciation for his efforts. I'd like to thank the faculty of the Prairie View A&M University History Department (specifically James T. Jones, Kenneth Howell, and Charles Grear) for accepting me as an equal colleague and believing in me as a scholar when they didn't have to.

I'd like to thank Dr. T. R. Williams, the brothers of the Deacon's Ministry, and rest of my Houston-based New Faith Church family for their kind and patient words of support.

To my parents, Benny and Betty Goodwin, and my brother Benny, Jr., there has never been a moment in my life when I didn't feel loved. For that, a million thank yous will never be enough. I love you guys. My most heartfelt expressions of thanks are saved for the ones who have put up with me over the years: my sons, Alexander and Bryce, and my long-suffering wife, Gwendolyn. All that I am is because of their unconditional love. If the Lord were to call me home today, I could rest peacefully knowing that I've been blessed with a family who loves me . . . in spite of me.

Lastly, this story would not be possible were it not for the professionalism and guidance I received from the State House Press and the McWhiney History Education Group, specifically Dr. Don Frazier, Amy Smith, Scott Clowdus, and Claudia Gravier Frigo. Your patience made this arduous process possible as the story evolved from concept to reality. Thank you very much.

I learned a long time ago that "all things are possible to him that believes." I have no idea what God has in store for my life, but I continually feel his presence around me and in my life. He is so awesome that I don't ever feel worthy of his love, blessing, and forgiveness.

It is always customary for authors to accept responsibilities for factual and/or contextual errors in their research; I will do likewise: Any errors contained in this manuscript are solely my responsibility.

REG

The LORD is my shepherd, I shall not want.
He makes me lie down in green pastures;
He leads me beside quiet waters.
He restores my soul; He guides me in the paths of righteousness
for His name's sake.
Even though I walk through the valley of the shadow of death,
I fear no evil, for You are with me;
Your rod and Your staff, they comfort me.
You prepare a table before me in the presence of my enemies;
You have anointed my head with oil; My cup overflows.
Surely goodness and loving kindness will follow me all the days
of my life, and I will dwell in the house of the LORD forever.
Psalm 23: 1–6

Look unto me, and be ye saved, all the ends of the earth;
For I am God, and there is none else.
Isaiah 45:22

PART ONE

The Government, the New Deal, and Aging Ex-Slaves

"If you wants to know 'bout slavery time, it was Hell."
 Carter J. Jackson

"Well, I'll do de best I can to tell yous 'bout my life. I used to have de good 'collection, but worriment 'bout ups and downs has 'fected my 'membrance."
 Scott Hooper

"We'uns had good times in slavery, but I likes my freedom."
 Henderson Perkins

ONE

THE WPA AND THE SLAVE NARRATIVES

By the 1930s there were new interpretations of the South, the Civil War, and slavery. Southern historians argued that slavery was a necessary evil in the civilizing of the savage black. Supported by Jim Crow racism, this position was accepted around the country by the time the stock market crashed in 1929. In his attempt to find employment for unemployed writers and other white-collar professionals, President Franklin D. Roosevelt endorsed a program that sent hundreds of mostly white women into the primarily black communities across the country in search of former slaves and their recollections of their lives as slaves. Many of those being interviewed hesitated in discussing the past, especially given the likely race of their interviewer, whereas others openly discussed what they remembered of their forced servitude. Unfortunately, historians initially ignored this Slaves' Narratives Project until the urban revolutions of the civil rights movement began tearing the country apart. As a result of the new self-awareness of the black community, a new generation of historians, both black and white, began mining the slaves' narratives for clues as to the lives of antebellum blacks and soon began challenging the perceptions that blacks were passive participants in their own lives.

There is no question that the Great Depression radically altered the economic and social structures of the United States. Perhaps more important than the tangible changes were the altered perceptions and expectations Americans had of their government. Even though the doctrine of rugged individualism had served Americans well up to that point, increasingly the displaced citizens looked to the government for answers. When Roosevelt assumed office in 1933, the nation's economy was in shambles. He not only faced the daunting task of restoring public confidence in government, especially the executive branch, but also with trying to improve the numerous socioeconomic problems associated with the worst economic crisis in the country's history. Interestingly, restoring public confidence in government was easy when compared to fixing the nation's economy.

Created as a division of the Works Progress Administration (WPA) in 1935, Federal Project Number One provided relief funds to unemployed white-collar workers (artists, actors, writers, and musicians) throughout the country. As a part of this, the Federal Writer's Project (FWP) was created to preserve US culture through the compilation of local and state guidebooks and other projects that focused on oral histories and folklore. Although cultural projects were not paramount in Roosevelt's New Deal policies, the distribution of relief funds to the unemployed was. At its height, the FWP provided employment to more than six thousand writers, editors, historians, and archivists who scoured their local communities creating a depression-era "snapshot" of the United States. These images and words documented the deprivation of the 1930s as experienced by Americans throughout the country regardless of gender and ethnicity.[1]

Perhaps one of the most referenced aspects of the FWP was the Slaves' Narrative Project. Whereas the Guides Series produced essays and books of local historical value, the Slaves' Narrative Project changed the paradigm in the historical analysis of slavery in this country by providing historians with firsthand accounts of events that were often misconstrued by other primary sources. As a result, many books and television documentaries have been based on their findings. Furthermore, the importance of the slaves narratives is that they provided former slaves the opportunity to tell *their* stories of life during slavery; stories that have been too often distorted by those wishing to downplay the obvious atrocities of the inhumane institution of slavery.

However, the study of former slaves did not begin with Roosevelt's New Deal. In the late 1920s, sociologists in Chicago were studying virtually every aspect of local black life in communities that were fast becoming identified as "ghettos." Charles S. Johnson contributed to these initial Chicago studies. Later, he created the Social Science Institute at Fisk University and replicated the Chicago studies by examining Nashville's black communities. While conducting these studies, his team invariably interviewed former slaves. Johnson soon recognized the value of these interviews in understanding the sociological aspects of slavery from the former slaves' perspective. Eventually, more than one hundred interviews from former slaves in rural Tennessee, Kentucky, and Alabama were published.[2]

Others were also interested in detailing the slaves' history. While teaching US history at Southern University in 1929, historian John Cade directed his students to find former slaves and talk to them about their memories of slavery. In discussing the direction of the project, Cade indicated, "Students were asked to seek information regarding food, clothing, housing facilities, working conditions, amusements, religious practices, educational opportunities, family life, punishments, and any other information obtainable."[3] Cade's successes at Southern University led him to replicate the process at Prairie View A&M University in the mid-1930s.

In 1935, Cade published his article, "Out of the Mouths of Ex-Slaves," which discussed slavery from the views of the surviving slaves. Greats like Carter G. Woodson, W. E. B. DuBois, Walter White, and Langston Hughes, who wrote about and espoused the views that African Americans were worth academic and literary examination, influenced Cade's work.[4]

The New Deal's FWP led to a broadening of Cade's methodology. The FWP provided the avenue for unemployed white-collar workers to preserve US culture through the biographies and folklore of hundreds of "average" Americans.[5] The FWP's Life Histories and American Guides projects succeeded in creating a social and historical profile of states, cities, localities, and people throughout the United States. John Lomax, recognized as one of the country's preeminent authorities on folklore, was asked to direct the folklore and folk histories component of the American Guides. In 1936, black writers assigned to the Florida Writer's Project interviewed former slaves as part of the process of collecting information on indigenous African American history and culture. In March 1937, these narratives of former slaves came to the attention of Lomax. In April 1937, the Slaves' Narratives Project was created, and Lomax distributed a memorandum establishing the guidelines for the interviewing of former slaves.

Lomax's guidelines included questions that were designed to gather responses regarding slave life and perceptions of current living conditions. Lomax cautioned interviewers to use those questions as guides and to refrain from too much prompting to achieve a desired response. He said, "It should be remembered that the Federal Writers' [P]roject is not interested in taking sides on any question. The worker should not censor any material collected, regardless of its nature."[6]

A July 1937 memorandum to state directors added more suggestions to the interview questions originally proposed by Lomax. These questions asked the former slaves to comment on their lives and experiences since the end of slavery, address their relationships with their children, identify the types of work they did since freedom, and explain how they were presently being supported. These questions provide a window into the lives of these former slaves as elderly individuals during the 1930s and offer a broader insight on blacks during the Great Depression. The interviews of former slaves occurred in seventeen states, including Alabama, Arkansas, Florida, Georgia, Indiana, Kansas, Kentucky, Maryland, Mississippi, Missouri, North Carolina, Ohio, Oklahoma, South Carolina, Tennessee, Texas, and Virginia, principally during 1937 and 1938.

In 1938, Benjamin A. Botkin replaced Lomax as the guiding force behind the collection of folklore and folk histories. Like Lomax, he also believed the Slaves' Narratives Project would be integral to African American and US history, "For the first and the last time, a large number of surviving slaves, (many of whom have since died), have been permitted to tell their own story, in their own way."[7]

In examining the slaves' narratives, many of the interviews are detailed, but others provide only cursory information. The interviewers, who were typically white, provided descriptions of the former slaves, sometimes in great detail. The individual narratives generally began with the former slave's name, place of birth, and the location of the interview. Furthermore, interviewers occasionally described the former slaves' physical condition, housing, and their assessment of the ex-slaves' ability to accurately recall important events or personal milestones.

At times, the interviewer's initial expectations and personal descriptions of the former slaves were dictated by racist perceptions. For example, some interviewers were surprised with the demeanor of the former slaves, whereas others freely used words such as *darkey, nigger, aunty,* and *uncle.*[8] For example, the interviewer of Mazique Sanco of San Angelo was surprised when he did not speak in what was typically considered the dialect of depression-era blacks.[9]

The interviewers of former slaves Susan Ross and "Uncle" Willis Anderson illustrated what historian John Blassingame called "rigid plantation etiquette."[10] Interviewed in Jasper, the interviewer of Ross focused his perceptions of her based on her perceived ancestry. He used information from Ross plus his own thoughts to fill in the blanks and noted, "Her skin color together with her secretive manner would point to Indian blood."[11] Interestingly, during the interview Ross commented that her mother believed *she* may have been part Indian. Ross apparently could not verify this, but the interviewer concluded that these factors indicated Indian ancestry without absolute proof. Likewise, the interviewer of Anderson of Centerville used the antebellum title of "Uncle" and described him as an "interesting character" with a "vivid" memory. This interviewer also commented that Anderson wore a hat during their conversation that made him look more "unique."[12]

The Texas interviews were conducted throughout the state, and former slaves from El Paso to Jasper and Corpus Christi to San Angelo participated. At the conclusion of the project in 1939, more than three hundred interviews were submitted to the national WPA offices. The original narrative interviews and other state WPA records were not sent to Washington, D.C., instead copies are housed in the Library of Congress because the Center for American History at the University of Texas in Austin maintains the originals. Nonetheless, it is difficult to ascertain the total number of former slaves interviewed because many of the state records were lost or discarded during World War II.

The Library of Congress holds 308 interviews of former slaves living in Texas during the Great Depression. Fifty-nine percent of those former slaves interviewed were men, 43 percent were born in Texas, and 3 percent did not indicate to their interviewer where they were born. The table indicates that of those former slaves born outside of Texas, the greatest percentage of them (49 percent) were born in Louisiana followed by Alabama (27 percent), Mississippi (18 percent), and Virginia (16 percent).[13] In addition to their birthplace, the former slaves also indicated their ages at the time of the interview. The average

age of men interviewed was eighty-seven years old, whereas the average age of women was slightly younger at eighty-five.

Percentage of Former Slaves Born Outside Texas

Louisiana	49
Alabama	27
Mississippi	18
Virginia	16
Tennessee	12
Georgia	11
Arkansas	6
Missouri	5
South Carolina	5
Kentucky	5
North Carolina	3
Africa	1
Florida	1
Indian Territory	1
Maryland	1
Ohio	1
Oklahoma	1
West Virginia	1

Despite the amount of information collected, many historians questioned the validity and reliability of the narratives. Historian Kenneth Stampp questioned whether the slaves had the capacity to retell their slave experiences. In *Rebels and Sambos* he wrote, "Direct evidence from the slaves themselves is hopelessly inadequate. Well over 90 percent of them were illiterate and even the small literate minority seldom found an opportunity to write or speak with candor."[14]

Likewise, Blassingame also questioned the value of ex-slaves' biographies and slaves' narratives but for different reasons. Blassingame argued that the ex-slaves' biographies were questionable, not because slaves did not have the capacity to retell their experiences, but because they were "frequently dictated to and written by whites."[15] He concluded that ex-slaves' biographies, particularly those from the nineteenth century, were merely abolitionist propaganda with little value of accurately portraying slavery or the lives of slaves.

Furthermore, Blassingame specifically criticized the WPA's Slaves Narratives Project. He argued that the narratives were fundamentally flawed for several reasons. First, he believed the interviewers were inexperienced and could not obtain "trustworthy" information from the former slaves. Secondly, Blassingame argued that many interviews were retold and revised by hand several times before they were typed, introducing the possibility of distortions and inaccuracies. Lastly, he questioned the ability of aged individuals to accurately recall events from their childhood.[16]

Many of the former slaves such as Josephine Ryles and James Smith admitted their memories of slavery were vague or that they were too young to remember slavery. Ryles, interviewed in Galveston, said her memory was not good because she was old. In fact, she joked that she was as old as the Gulf of Mexico.[17] Likewise Smith of Palestine stated that he was only five years old when emancipated and was too young to recall specific events of slavery. Nonetheless, Smith indicated that it was his mother who told him where the family was originally from, where he was born, and stories about slavery.[18] Similarly, Patsy Moses and Walter Leggett also recalled stories about slavery told to them by their parents and grandparents.[19]

However, throughout the narratives there were those former slaves that indicated an ability to recall past events with amazing clarity. Abram Sells of Jamestown was able to provide the names, some pertinent information, and ages at death of his great-grandfather, grandfather, and both parents.[20] Henry Lewis of Pine Island (Jefferson County) vividly recalled the names of his owners, the location of their plantations, one in Louisiana and the other in Jefferson County, Texas, as well as the names and ages at death of his grandmother and mother.[21] Callie Shepard of Dallas was proud of her ability to remember and relate stories from her childhood. When the interviewer asked her if she could tell them about slavery, she replied, "Course I kin tell you. I got 'memberance like dey don't have nowadays. Dat 'cause things is goin' round and round too fast without no settin' and talkin' things over."[22]

As stated, some historians questioned the validity of the slaves narratives and ex-slaves' biographies because of the biases of the projects' editors; however, more intriguing is the possibility that the former slaves themselves selectively edited their memories when responding to the questions. After all, the former slaves were raised in an environment in which blacks distrusted and felt inferior to whites. As a result, even in their old age, the conditioning of inferiority was still evident. Throughout the Texas Slave Narratives, the former slaves still reverently referred to their former owners as *massa*, *marster*, and *missus*. This form of respect was still evident in how some of the former slaves reacted to their interviewers. For example, Mandy Morrow of Georgetown referred to her white interviewer as "massa."[23]

Conversely, there were several instances in which it was apparent that former slaves often distrusted whites. In his recollections of slavery, former slave and abolitionist Frederick Douglass emphatically stated that most slaves were conditioned to lie and omit details when asked about slavery.[24] In Texas, Julia Blanks of San Antonio clearly described for the interviewer the names and occupations of three of her four children. Of the fourth child, she merely said, "And I have one boy here." Blanks simply chose to omit details about this last son from the discussion.[25] Wes Brady of Marshall, indicated his memory was fine, but he commented that whites did not want to hear the truth about slavery.[26] This belief obviously dictated the way some of the former slaves related to their white interviewers. Martin Jackson of San Antonio, like Douglass, commented that former slaves rarely talked about their slave experiences in public.

> Lots of old slaves closes the door before they tell the truth about their days of slavery. When the door is open, they tell how kind their masters was and how rosy it all was. You can't blame them for this, because they had plenty of early discipline, making them cautious about saying anything uncomplimentary about their masters.[27]

Jackson also made inquiries of the interviewer even before he confirmed his identity and consented to the interview. He wanted to know who the interviewer was, who directed the interviewer to him in the first place, and which federal agency was directing the interviews.[28]

Such suspicion was also evident in the interview with former slave Millie Manuel. Manuel agreed with Jackson in that she feared retaliation after talking openly about slavery. She became confrontational when asked to take a picture and said, "Me get my picture taken and get arrested? No, I won't have no picture taken. No, I don't care what yo' say. I wouldn't trust a white man no more that a rattler."[29]

Likewise, Felix Haywood, age ninety-two and blind, of San Antonio was initially depicted as "whimsical," but before the interview began, Haywood asked the interviewer if he was white or black. The interviewer responded "black" probably assuming that Haywood may not talk to him if he admitted to being white. However, the interviewer said that Haywood laughed and said,

Felix Haywood

> No, you ain't. I knowed you was a white man when you came up the path and speaks. I jus' always asks that question for fun. I makes white men a little insulted when you don't knows they is white, and it makes niggers all conceited up when you think maybe they is white.[30]

Although there were instances of hesitation in discussing their former lives, the ex slaves provided invaluable information that shed light on the lives of those once considered unfit to enjoy the benefits of a free society. Nonetheless, the FWP, Federal Project Number One, and the WPA were popular targets of the New Deal's congressional opponents, especially Martin Dies and the House Un-American Activities Committee (HUAC). Dies fought to withdraw funding from any New Deal program he believed supported Communist subversion in the United States. Along with conservative allies in the House and Senate, Dies successfully pressured Roosevelt into scaling back many of Federal Project Number One's programs by the late 1930s. The FWP lost its funding in October 1939 because of political pressures and the increases in the defense budget after the start of World War II. However, the functions of the FWP were transferred to the individual states, and many of the projects continued until April 1943.

When the federal government ceased financial support of the FWP, local governments and private entities sponsored activities that continued gathering the slave's experiences and made them available to the public. After serving as the initial force behind the national Slaves' Narrative Project, Lomax contracted with the Library of Congress to travel throughout the South recording various genres of folk songs. In the early 1940s, John, his wife Ruby Lomax, and sons John, Jr., and Alan conducted and tape recorded additional interviews with former slaves. One of these interviews was with "Uncle" Billy McCrea of Jasper. Interestingly, McCrea was questioned about his recollections of slavery as part of the initial WPA interviews in 1937.[31]

However, this second interview with McCrea provided more detailed information and provided historians more information about his slave experiences and other aspects of his life. Furthermore, the recordings, themselves, are invaluable in that they provide the ability to hear the interviewer's questions and subsequently McCrea's responses. On more than one occasion during the interview, the audible reactions of amazement and awe from the interviewers to stories of slavery can be heard. Additionally, the Lomaxes could also be heard singing along as McCrea sang folk songs.[32]

The original Texas slaves' narratives were eventually catalogued along with the other seventeen states' narratives under the direction of Benjamin Botkin. The first widespread distribution of the slaves' narratives occurred in 1945 when Botkin assembled the approximately 2,300 narratives and published *Lay My Burden Down*. Nonetheless, historians virtually ignored them until Norman Yetman wrote his article "The Background of the Slave Narrative Collection," and George Rawick published the edited collection, *From Sundown to Sunup*. Since then, historians have accepted the narratives as valid primary sources and now seek to find new ways to use them.[33]

The narratives of former slaves have provided historians and sociologists with a wealth of information regarding the lives of blacks during slavery and the Great Depression. Although many of the slave narratives implied the atmosphere of "plantation etiquette," they nonetheless succeeded in presenting black life as seen through black eyes.

TWO

REMEMBERING SLAVERY IN TEXAS

The history of Texas is filled with stories of wars and conquests. All Texas children know the stories of David Crockett, William Travis, and Sam Houston and their struggles to free the state from what they believed was the tyrannical rule of a Mexican dictator. But how many Texas children have been introduced to the stories of Hannah Scott, Campbell Davis, or Annie Little? And yet the history of Texas's slaves deserves to be known and understood for what they accomplished despite their lives of bondage and racial segregation. The voices of the ex-slaves convey a uniqueness of experiences not seen anywhere else in the known world at any time in history. In Texas these stories can finally be placed within the proper context of illustrating what antebellum Texas society was like for all Texans, black and white, free and slave.

Texas is a Southern state. The proliferation of Southerners in Texas during the antebellum years suggests they had a tremendous influence in the development of slavery in the state. Furthermore, evidence suggests that the form of slavery that appeared in Texas was unique compared to other slave states by the time the Abraham Lincoln became president. First of all, Texas was the only slave state that bordered on a foreign country in 1860. As a result, Texas slave owners were just as concerned about their slaves escaping south into Mexico as they were about them escaping north. Secondly, the topography of Texas confined slavery to the east and southeastern portions of the state because the rest was unsuitable for the traditional cultivation of slavery-related crops.[1]

By the 1930s many former black slaves remembered their lives when someone else took care of their every need, whereas others only recalled the brutality and degradation of slavery. Why would a former slave still living in Texas believe slavery was an acceptable condition? This is the question historians have been asking for many years. However, many of those asking the question will never understand what it is like to be humiliated in front of their children, or watch helplessly as their wives and daughters are raped. Some argue that the victims of the Holocaust are qualified to answer such questions, but the reality is that tragedy lasted only a few years, not generations. Nonetheless, it is apparent that many of the former black slaves were cautious about answering questions asked by whites they did not know. As a result, they may have merely responded to the inquiries in a manner they believed the interviewer wanted to hear. Others feared losing their meager government pensions if they openly criticized whites. Still, many former slaves brazenly commented about the brutalities of slavery.

Slavery in Texas has not received the scholarly attention when compared to other slave states. Still, slavery has been a part of Texas since the first expeditions of the Spanish conquistadores. Even when the US Congress was considering the question of slavery in Missouri and the remainder of the Louisiana Territories and before Stephen F. Austin began US colonization, slavery existed.[2]

After Mexico gained its independence from Spain, Moses Austin convinced the government to allow his colonization of Texas. His son, Stephen, eventually led the "Old Three Hundred" into Texas after his death. Like the previous Spanish government, the Mexican government believed slavery was immoral but nonetheless realized the importance of slave labor to Texas' growing agricultural economy. As a result, there were five thousand slaves in Texas by 1836, located mostly along the Brazos, Colorado, and Trinity Rivers in the southeast part of the state. The battle for Texas's independence removed the last remaining obstacles that prevented slavery from its full potential. Southerners believed slave labor would produce high economic profits if supported by favorable governmental policies. As a result, slavery increased as Texas became economically dependent on cotton and slave labor.[3]

Historian Randolph Campbell argued that slavery came to Texas with Austin's initial settlers and soon became an integral part of the local economy well before the move for independence in 1836. Still, he contends that slavery was not a solidified part of Texas because Mexico could have attracted settlers without allowing slavery. But because of the Mexican government's vacillation on the subject and Austin's persuasiveness, the Mexican government stood by and allowed slave-produced cotton to become so profitable that Southerners came by the hundreds after the 1830s. In addition to those located adjacent to the Brazos, Colorado, and Trinity Rivers, slaves were also found in concentrations near Nacogdoches and in communities along the Red River.[4]

By the 1850s, slavery and cotton production became interlaced. The slave population increased by nearly 125,000, and cotton production increased from slightly more than 58,000 bales per year in 1850 to nearly 183,000 bales per year in 1860. The commitment to cotton production coincided with the commitment to slave labor. Furthermore, Texas's slave owners realized the positive relation between the number of slaves and the ability to increase cotton production.[5]

Even with the increase in the number of slaves in Texas, by 1855 the black population, slave and free, was mostly confined to eighty-two counties. A majority, slightly more than seven thousand, of the state's black population was found in Harrison County. Conversely, Cooke County listed only one black, a slave. Generally, the demographic census indicated that blacks were typically found in the eastern half of Texas. By 1857, Texas's northeast counties had more than 25,000 slaves, with Harrison, Bowie, and Cass counties listing the majority of slaves.[6]

Generally speaking, the average slave owner owned at least ten slaves.[7] However, there were exceptions. For example, the Downs family plantation near Waco maintained about one hundred slaves. Evidence indicates that these bondsmen were also treated poorly and that the treatment of slaves on central Texas plantations was generally severe, especially when the owner hired an overseer. Although they were charged with ensuring daily production, many overseers enjoyed the power the whip gave them. They often drove slaves unmercifully, and "nearly every hour of the day had some of them across the barrel lashing them."[8]

And the treatment of slaves in Texas was not that different from other Southern states. For example, slaves were denied the right to own individual property, buy or sell goods, carry a firearm, and forbidden from testifying against a white man in court. The most important aspect of the slave's life was his obedience to the will of his white master.[9] It was the need to maintain this obedience that led the plantation elite to develop a culture that kept blacks in a specific sociological and political place in Southern culture. This place became the underclass of society.

Further, the Texas culture created by white Southerners depended on various systems designed to control not only the movements of blacks, but also practically every aspect of their lives. Perhaps the most obvious manifestation of black control was the violence committed against the black community. Violence, specifically the act of physical violence, was an unfortunate part of every slave's existence.[10] Southern states created laws that gave slave owners the right to punish their slaves in whatever manner they deemed appropriate. In some case this included death.[11] Even when heinous acts were committed in which other slaves were witnesses, the Southern courts would not take the word of a black man against that of a white man, a trend that continued well into the twentieth century.[12] This created an environment in which slaves understood there would be no recourse for acts committed on their person by the slave owner or any of his hired agents (overseers or drivers).[13] Many simply acquiesced. Others, however, retaliated physically against their abusers, and still others chose to run away.

The most consistent question asked of the former slaves involved their remembrances and perceptions of their former conditions in bondage in the antebellum environment. Although this may seem to be a simple and direct query, the answers were most often influenced by multiple factors not easily understood. Most often, the former slaves responded to questions of their former bondage based in part on their remembrances of how they were treated in relation to their work. It is no surprise then that those who were house slaves tended to remember slavery, and their owners, more fondly than those who labored in the fields. However, there were those whose recollections and perceptions of their lives as slaves were tempered by their current living conditions in the 1930s. For some of the former slaves, surviving slavery was an easier task compared to the challenges they faced as elderly individuals in the Great Depression.

Texas was, and remains, a Southern state. Most of the white immigrants to Texas during the antebellum era were from Southern states and brought their understanding of slavery and the supposed proper relationship between the races with them, which means that slavery in Texas was no different than what might have been found in the other populous slave states throughout the South.[14]

Born some time around 1855 on a plantation near Whitesville, North Carolina, Walter Leggett and his family belonged to a Captain Burns and his family. He apparently did not experience harsh treatment from the captain, but he told the interviewer that his parents nonetheless said Burns was "mean and whipped them and make them work like dogs." But Leggett's experiences may have been different from that of his parents because he was a house slave with the responsibility for caring for Burns' son. However, Leggett recalled that Sundays were a special time for the slaves on the Burns plantation because they were allowed to have church services and on Saturdays they ate, drank, and danced.[15]

Jack and Rosa Maddox were both born into slavery and neither one knew their actual birth date. Jack belonged to the Maddox family from Georgia, whereas Rosa belonged to the Andrews family in Mississippi. They married in Union Parish, Louisiana, in 1869, which meant that at the time of their interview they had been married for sixty-nine years. The Andrews family owned twelve slaves and Rosa said they were treated well. "Dr. Andrews was good to us and give us good li'l cabins and cotton mattresses and blankets. We had enough to eat, too." At the age of nine, Rosa went to work in the house as "waitin' and nursegirl" to Dr. Andrews's children and wife, who she called "Miss Fannie."[16]

Others, such as William Paxton, Clarissa Scales, and Leggett, remembered slavery with varying degrees of fondness. Paxton said he experienced few whippings, and stated, "dere wasn't much whippin' only when de slaves was lazy," and "Marse Paxton and de boys was mighty good to de slaves."[17] Similarly, Scales, whose job was "tenden the fires and herdin' hawgs," recalled the benevolence of William Vaughn toward her family. "Master Vaughn was good and treated us all right. Missy's name was Margaret, and she was good too."[18] However, Leggett boldly told his WPA interviewer that, "I like slavery just fine, in fact, I ain't got no use for free niggers. I don't know who is going to take keer of them when they gets old. The free niggers think they are sho' smart. I ain't got no use for churches, women and free niggers—they make the difference between this country being a hell and a heaven." He also indicated his disdain for religion when he said, "church folks used to have a good times; singings and dinner on the grounds. All they do now is ask for money. I ain't no 'ligous man."[19]

Mary Reynolds said her owners, the Kilpatricks, allowed her father, Tom Vaughn, a free-born black man, to live on the plantation to be near his wife and child. She recalled that her father built pianos in New York and Chicago, and he was persuaded to move south because "he could find a lot of work to do with pianos in them parts." When asked about slavery, Reynolds replied that it was "the worst days ever seed in the world." She also said that she had many scars on her old frail body that served as constant reminders of how atrocious slavery was.[20]

Perhaps because of her lighter complexion, eighty-four-year-old Sarah Allen said she enjoyed the paternalism of the plantation. Still, she acknowledged, "It's a pretty hard story, how cruel some of the marsters was, but I had the luck to be with good white people. . . . . You know in slavery times when people had bad marsters dey would run away but we didn't want to."[21]

Laura Moore also experienced good treatment as a slave. Described by the WPA interviewer as an "old fashioned darky" she was eighty-six years old and referred to slavery as "de most peaceful and happy time dat was." She further said that her fondness for slavery caused her severe distress with other blacks, including her own family, because "colored people today know nothing about de good part of slavery." Moore told the interviewer that she and the other slaves of the Tippen's plantation "got everythin' give to us. If you gets anythin' out of it from people nowdays, you got to slave worse than we did." Finally, Moore said that she did not believe blacks were friendly and actually preferred the company of "Mexican folks. . . . niggers call me a slavery nigger. My grand-chillen thinks it is smart 'cause dey can read. Dats all dey can do—dat and dance. There's other things they don't know and when I tells 'em what it is they laugh and have no manners."[22]

Even though there was the constant fear of the whip, Marshall Showers still remembered the safety and security of plantation life, "I like de old times best. Den I has plenty to eat and good clothes and a good time." Showers' recollections of slavery may have been slanted by his present condition of life during the 1930s' depression when many, regardless of race, suffered from hunger and homelessness. Although he commented that he had a "good time," Showers later remembered that there were severe repercussions for any violation, real or imagined, of plantation etiquette. He said there was little hesitation on the part of the owner or overseer to punish a slave that they considered disobedient. "You sass his wif an' de stakes you face down on de ground. Den dey takes down you britches an' cuts your ass all to pieces wid a bull whip." He further indicated the owners' wives exercised a great deal of power over the slaves, even if they sometimes fabricated information that would lead to a slave being punished. "Times de boss' wife she make up stories 'bout you, say you lazy, say you hides out, say you sass 'er when you ain't done it. Den dey stakes you out again an' de ole bull whip make de blood fly."[23]

Another former slave, Emma Countee Wilson, also believed slavery was beneficial to blacks. She was eighty-five years old at the time of her interview and described in the narrative as an "unusually handsome Negro." Wilson, raised as a "house gal" with her mother as the family cook, said her owner provided them plenty of food. Additionally, Wilson said, "Marse Russel was good to the slaves. Dey has heaps to eat but dey ain't got no money. De marster neve 'lows any of us to read a book."[24]

Martin Jackson's narrative was indicative of those that were somehow contradictory in nature. Such interviews usually began by commenting how benign slavery was but concluded by indicating awareness of slaves who were horrifically punished. Jackson's narrative began by claiming that slavery was a "godsend" for blacks. In fact, he believed that without slavery blacks might regress to the savagery racists normally identified with Africa. Jackson told the interviewer, "Our 20 million Negroes are descended from four million sent over from Africa. If it had not been for the slave traffic, we would still be heathens. Out of bad comes good and out of good, I'm afraid, is going to come bad. The colored man is going to lose his strength and natural cunning, and he is going to slide downhill faster than the American white man—and that's fast enough."

Jackson then turned philosophical about slavery and confessed a belief that it was a degrading system, more so for the slave owner than for the slave. He believed that those who survived slavery were more than likely to say their former masters were kind or that they were treated well rather than tell the truth because they still feared the repercussions that could be inflicted on them by local whites, even in the 1930s. He stated that early slave indoctrination included intense discipline, which punished blacks for saying anything negative about whites or slavery. The truth, according to Jackson, was that blacks suffered tremendously under slavery and that most blacks would not want to live as slaves, regardless of what they might say to their white interviewers.[25]

Therefore, the absolute honesty of those participating in the slaves' narratives could be questioned as to their veracity. Many answered that they were not treated well. However, others did comment that their treatment was so good that they wished they were still slaves so their former masters could take care of them again.[26]

It is also worth noting that many of the comments found throughout the Texas narratives hint that it was not slavery that these aged individuals remembered fondly. Instead it was the times of being cared for by someone else and not having the burden of caring for oneself as an elderly person in the midst of poverty and uncertainty of the 1930s. There were several comments referring to food and hunger, which implied that these elderly people were not adequately able to care for themselves. As slaves they benefited from the paternalism of the master, and if they were productive field hands they were treated accordingly. The perceptions offered in the narratives were indicative of the times in which the ex-slaves lived, and not the times they were recalling from memory.

It does leave one to wonder if the answers in response to their treatment as slaves was the result of years of conditioning or if as elderly individuals in the 1930s they were often alone and hungry. Frederick Douglass believed the indoctrination of slavery would prevent a former slave from saying anything that could be perceived as negative toward whites. "They suppress the truth rather than take the consequences of telling it, and in doing so prove themselves a part of the human family. If they have anything to say of their masters, it is generally in their master's favor, especially when speaking to an untried man."[27]

Thus, the perceptions of former slaves and that of their WPA interviewers are what they are. A distance of seventy years may not have been enough time to allow slaves to truly tell an unfamiliar person, white or black, how they were treated under slavery. Further, the record may be distorted because of that or it may be distorted because of their present living conditions during the depression. Either way, it is clear that a slave's perception of slavery was a result of their experiences throughout his or her life and not just during slavery.

Give thanks to the LORD, for He is good;
For His loving kindness is everlasting.
Psalm 188:1

PART TWO

Masters and Slaves

How and for what causes were the slaves punished? Did the slaves ever run away to the North?

"My marster and mistress was good to all de slaves dat worked for dem. But our overseer, Jimmy Shearer, was sho' mean."
    Mrs. John Barclay

"My master was a Frenchman and was real mean to me. He run a saloon and kept bad women. I don't know nothing 'bout my folks, if I even had any, 'cept mama. They done tell me she was a bad woman and a French Creole."
    Frank Bell

"I allus lived in de house with the white folks and ate at their table when they was through, and slep' on the floor."
    Lizzie Jones

"I didn't know how to git out of dere, but I's gwine north where dere ain't no slaveowners."
    Thomas Cole

"I seed a man run away and de white men got de dogs and dey kotch him and put him in de front room and he jump through de big window and break de glass all up. Dey sho' whips him when dey kotches him."
    Sarah Ashley

THREE

THE MASTER

There is little question that the antebellum economies of Texas, and the South in general, depended on the abilities of the owner or one of his agents to make sure slaves completed their daily production quota. When that quota was met, evidence indicates that slaves enjoyed the benevolent protection of their master. However, owners and overseers did not hesitate in using the whip or other forms of punishments when they believed slaves were either loafing or exhibiting unruly behavior. Unfortunately, there is little evidence suggesting the frequency of whippings that occurred on Texas plantations, and what we do know about plantation violence comes from the ex-slaves themselves and that it had a definite effect on their perceptions of slavery.[1]

There are stories told that illustrate how any perceived or real acts of disobedience could result in severe punishments or even death. For example, a newspaper article reported that a local white man shot and killed a slave he believed to be a thief. Interestingly, the article further indicated that the following morning that it was discovered that this particular slave had in fact murdered the overseer on the nearby Burdett Plantation just hours before he was subsequently killed.[2]

Another newspaper article indicated that a local overseer working on the Dawson Plantation was found guilty of the death of a female slave. Although the article did not comment on the supposed crime of the female slave, witnesses claimed the overseer "whipped the slave until she fell dead." Even though he was arrested, the overzealous overseer escaped from custody and attempts to reacquire him were not forthcoming.[3]

Hannah Scott, one of nine slaves belonging to "White Pa," was generally treated well and recalled that White Pa was "mighty good to the black folks." However, White Pa and his wife were "poor folk" and eventually were forced to sell their slaves to Bat Peterson as payment for outstanding debts. Unlike White Pa, Peterson was a mean taskmaster and worked the slaves from "daylight till nine o'clock at night."[4]

Scott remembered "'Bout nin o'clock dey hollers 'cotton up' and dat de quittin' signal. We goes to de quarters and jes drap on de bunk and go to sleep without nothin' to eat." However, she indicated that the slaves typically had "plenty to eat and clothes, but dat all." When it appeared as though slavery might end in Arkansas, Peterson relocated to Richmond, Texas, to avoid emancipating his slaves.[5]

Millie Manuel was born near San Antonio and belonged to the Childers family who owned three slaves: herself and her parents. She also told how she was beat by the Childers "all of de time." When asked her why she received such harsh treatment, she replied "jes cos they could, I guess. They're all dead now and I's a-livin' and waitin' for glory; and when I go I won't be seein' any of them. And the Lord has spared me and he didn't spare them. They is gone where the Good Shepard has sent them to be slaves for the devil."[6] In addition to the whippings, Manuel indicated the Childers barely fed her and her family. "We didn't have food of no-account—no meat or nothin', just milk, and we would get a-hold of a egg once in a while. Us and the hogs got what milk they couldn't eat. We never had nothin' that was happy."[7]

Others had similar experiences to Manuel. Lulu Wilson also mentioned that her family barely had enough food to eat. Too often, all they received was "one li'l slice of sowbelly and a puny li'l piece of bread and a 'tater. I never had 'nough to stave the nongreness [hungriness] out'n my belly." Albert Todd said that his second owner barely fed her slaves. They would receive, "one sausage and one biscuit in the morning and nothin' else all day."[8]

Slavery was definitely ingrained in Texas economic and social culture. Even those who commented they had "good" masters remembered those who were beaten unmercifully. Slavery was a brutal system, but there is evidence that some slave owners treated their chattel with some modicum of respect as long as they obeyed. However, these same individuals still punished those who dared disobey or challenge their authority.

As a result, the interactions between masters and slaves generally dominated most discussions of slavery. Were masters mean or kind? Were the slaves hard workers or shiftless and lazy? These types of questions tended to justify and define the master–slave relationship based on the demeanor of the slave. If he or she was hard working, then the master responded with benevolent kindness. On the other hand, if he or she was lazy or thought to be a troublemaker, then the master was "forced" to use methods to correct what was perceived to be unacceptable behavior. Such thinking placed the blame of harsh treatment on the slave rather than the master. Nineteenth-century Southern historians argued that masters only resorted to the whip as a last resort. Slaves' narratives contradict this. Perhaps this is one reason why these historians eagerly discounted the records of former slaves because they disagreed with the image of the kind and compassionate master that they were presenting as a representation of the New South.

Albert Todd

Arguably the most difficult problem facing white slave owners was the discipline and control of black slaves. Although plantations varied in size and product and plantation owners varied in their treatment of slaves, most agreed that several factors needed to be present to maintain sufficient control. These included a careful balance of strict discipline and a belief in the biological inferiority of blacks, coupled with their own sense of righteous power.[9]

Abolitionist Angelina Grimké Weld commented that many white slave owners were purposely unaware of the day-to-day lives of their black slaves. Such pretended ignorance allowed them to remain emotionally detached from the blacks who made their lives easier and to punish them unmercifully at their whim.[10] Still, it was strict discipline, as exercised by the slave owners or the overseers, which was the most prevalent means of gaining and maintaining effective control. For example, one of Ashbel Smith's overseers indicated that the best way to get and maintain control over black slaves was through rigid discipline and frequent punishments.[11]

There are numerous instances throughout the South where some whites used any excuse to exercise their power of unabashed discipline on their slaves, often brutally, as an example to others.[12] In those rare instances in which there were laws protecting blacks from overly zealous masters, they were seldom enforced. In fact, it was nearly impossible for a white man to be convicted for any act of violence against a black man.[13]

Furthermore, it was generally accepted that punishments for minor infractions, such as perceived laziness or other general forms of misconduct, were left to the master. Whereas many states established laws for what was considered crimes against society, such as miscegenation or rape, other infractions were under the purview of the master to deal with in any manner he deemed appropriate.

However, on those rare occasions when discipline was lacking, it was typically because of the white master. Even though narratives and other surviving records indicates that the owners punished their slaves, sometimes severely, overseers were also known for their viciousness as well. In 1852, an overseer indicated to a slave owner that he was forced to kill an armed slave with a knife and would do so again if placed in a similar situation in which he feared for his own life.[14] Ex-slave Mary Reynolds also indicated that it was the overseer, who she referred to as Solomon, and not her owner Dr. Kilpatrick, who would often beat the black slaves. In fact, he would beat them so severely that Reynolds remembered that he could cut the flesh almost to the offender's bones. Her memories of this man and what he was allowed to do to the black men and women under his authority still made her angry. "I know that Solomon is burnin' in hell today and it pleasures me to know it. An' though they was good white folks that I heard tell of, I think they is plenty mo' of them in hell too."[15]

Evidence, black and white, generally illustrated that whippings were the usual form of punishments. However, there is little indication as to the frequency with which blacks were whipped in Texas, but one overseer said that he whipped slaves only as a last resort after several warnings.[16] Was this the exception or the rule in Texas? It is still difficult to prove one way or the other. Nonetheless, black slaves were whipped frequently. One commented that they were beaten often, especially when they failed to keep up with their daily production quotas, which was then followed by the application of salt on the open wounds.[17] Campbell Davis also said his owner routinely beat his sister and uncle for lack of production. Whenever his sister did not "spin 'nough," she would be stripped to the waist, instructed to lay on the ground on her stomach, and he would "lash her with a rawhide quirt." Likewise, whenever her Uncle Lewis did not pick enough cotton he was also told to lie on the ground so he could be whipped unmercifully.[18] Agatha Babino said her owner was "bad" and brutally beat his slaves. "He beat us till we bleed. He rub salt and pepper in. One time I sweep de yard. Young miss come home from college. She slap my face. She want to beat me. Mama say to beat her, so dey did. She took de beatin' for me. My Aunt run off 'cause dey beat her so much. Dey brung her back and beat her some more."[19]

In Texas, the power to administer discipline was also protected by law. In his detailed examination of slavery in Texas, Randolph Campbell found that white slave owners could legally punish their black slaves. For example, the master had the right to expect and demand obedience and submission from his slave. Former slave William Byrd commented that whenever a slave was "mean," his owner Master Sam Byrd administered "fifty licks over a log the first time and seventy-five licks the second time and 'bout that time he most gen'rally had a good nigger."[20]

Secondly, slave owners had the legal right to punish their slaves (men, women, and children), even to the point of death, without suffering legal repercussions. Abolitionist Weld found that whites not only had this power to treat another human being with vicious callousness in Texas, but also throughout the South. She commented on the horrid death of a young woman at the hands of her master: "A slaveholder, after flogging a little girl about thirteen years old, set her on a table with her feet fastened to a pair of stocks. He then locked the door and took out the key. When the door was opened she was found dead, having fallen from the table."[21] Then Weld indicated that this abomination went unpunished. One ex-slave in Texas reported that her father, who she believed had never been punished before for anything, was shot by their white owner without provocation.[22] Texas law also gave slave owners the right to punish their slaves as the "exclusive judge of the necessity for such correction; and the resistance by the slave, under such circumstances, if it results in homicide, renders him guilty of murder."[23]

Even though Campbell found there were laws that prevented slave owners from excessive cruelty, all too often, such brutality went unpunished. For example, Ben Simpson, who more than seventy years after emancipation, still feared the power of whites to punish those blacks who dared to complain about their treatment. As a result, he hesitatingly told his WPA interviewer how his master killed someone in Georgia, and to escape the local authorities, he moved his family and their slaves to Texas. Simpson also remembered how his mother was brutally shot by their owner on this journey because she failed to keep up. He said, "Mother, she give out on the way, 'bout the line of Texas. Her feet got raw and bleedin' and her legs swoll plumb out of shape. Then massa, he jus' take out he gun and shot her, and whilst she lay dyin' he kicks her two, three times and say, 'Damn a nigger what can't stand nothin'.'" Simpson further commented that he was not even permitted to bury her.[24]

Even with all of the brutality associated with whites and their management of their slaves, some white slave owners actually believed their role in the master–slave relationship was purely paternalistic in every sense of the word. Historian Eugene Genovese described this tenuous relationships as one in which both were inexplicably linked together.[25] "Cruel, unjust, exploitative, oppressive, slavery bound two peoples together in bitter antagonism while creating an organic relationship so complex and ambivalent that neither could express the simplest human feelings without reference to the other."[26]

Although slavery was a form of labor, for it to be as successful as it obviously was, there was something more. Genovese believed this something more was the growth of the master's paternalistic obligation toward the hapless slave. He further believed that it was the end of the overseas slave trade that actually contributed to this paternalistic environment found on most plantations. Masters found themselves forced to closely monitor the reproduction of slaves. "Of all the slave societies in the New World, that of the Old South alone maintained a slave force that reproduced itself. Less than 400,000 imported Africans had, by

1860, become a US black population of more than four million."[27] As a result, acts of paternalism and benevolence became necessary to allow the white ruling class to justify the enslavement on an entire race of people to build a successful economy that would have otherwise surely failed.

Other studies found the patriarchal relationship between master and slave was most prominent among those who had intimate, or close, contact with their slaves. These particular masters rarely lived away from the plantation and carefully considered the care of the slave's health and morals in keeping with their religious upbringing. Not only were the masters involved in the welfare of the slaves but also the children and spouses. The children typically worked in the fields alongside the adult slaves and overseers, whereas the wives often found themselves in charge of making slave clothing, supervising slave meals, and the care of sick and elderly.[28]

In Texas, many ex-slaves said they remembered experiencing the paternalism and benevolence of their former masters described by Genovese. Some former slaves believed they earned the respect of their white owners and that allowed them to enjoy special privileges most other black slaves did not. Will Adams told the story how his owner even took the word of his slave father, the plantation's driver, when he was questioned by a white neighbor.[29] However, there were differing testimonies in other slave narratives about the paternal master–slave relationship. During his interview, Eli Coleman initially commented that his owners, George Brady and his wife, treated their slaves well. "Massa Brady, he was one those jolly fellows and a real good man, allus good to his black folks. Missy, she was plumb angel." Later in the interview, Coleman told how this "real good man" treated those slaves who did not produce the day's quota. "Massa whopped a slave if he got stubborn or lazy." Coleman continued to tell of a particular slave who obviously objected to being beat and threatened to kill this "real good man." Coleman told how Brady chained this slave by the neck and feet to a tree every night for three weeks. In the end, Coleman said Brady's tactics worked. "After three weeks massa turnt him loose and that the proudes' nigger in the world, and the hardes' workin' nigger massa had after that."[30]

Furthermore, white slave owners, especially those without overseers or drivers, often meted out punishments whenever production quotas were not met personally.[31] Davis told how his owner, Henry Hood, employed a black

Van Moore

driver, but administered punishments personally and liberally. When punishing his slaves, Hood would instruct them to lie down on the ground and whipped them on their bare backs with a rawhide whip. Davis said he witnessed his uncle being beaten and remembered that he remained motionless on the ground as the whip cut into his flesh. He said his uncle did not move and found out later that he remained motionless because he was too afraid of Hood and feared he would receive worse punishments if he did.[32]

Owners who believed in punishing slaves for their lack of production did not care if they were males or females. In fact, sometimes being pregnant did not excuse slave women from their assigned duties.[33] For example, Van Moore recalled a pregnant slave being forced to lie in a special pit, one dug deep enough to accommodate her stomach, and was severely beaten on her bare back. As a result of one such beating, this woman became emotionally unstable.[34]

Often the successful management of black slaves became more than what one man could handle. In these situations, they hired professional overseers or promoted trusted black slaves to the position of driver. At no time did the master consider the possibility that the slaves could manage themselves without some form of personal oversight or oversight from an appointed agent.[35]

On the smaller plantations, the master typically managed their slaves personally, especially when most slave owners possessed ten slaves or fewer.[36] Overseers were typically not found unless the master owned more than twenty slaves.[37] Because overseers were notorious for their brutal treatment, slaves on plantations *with* overseers generally reported the greatest amount of brutality.[38]

Furthermore, brutality was associated with professional overseers because they were caught in an awkward position within the plantation's hierarchy. They did not have the prestige or the wealth to be plantation owners themselves, and slaves recognized their lack of respectability within the white world and often attempted to use it against the overseer. Professional overseers understood that the only way they would get and maintain respectability was through the use of force, often through *excessive* use of force. As a result, slaves respected their masters but despised the overseer.[39]

Although they may have been despised, overseers nevertheless maintained authority and respect through fear and intimidation.[40] Still, whenever a slave considered himself overly burdened by the techniques of the overseer, they might appeal to the master directly. Such actions were a constant reminder to the overseer that his only respect from the slave community depended on his ability to maintain slave productivity. Furthermore, his only authority came from the planter class, a social group that he was not allowed to enter. There were times when a master might dismiss an overseer for excessive cruelty, but the profits of a successful plantation generally outweighed the feelings of slaves.[41]

However, whenever overseers were employed on the plantation, it was the field slaves that were most often the ones on the receiving end of harsh treatment.[42] Ninety-seven-year-old Lulu Wilson said she was beaten often and severely by the master and the overseers. "They'd nearly beat us to death."[43]

Unfortunately, physical punishments were not the only means used by overseers to exercise control. Andy Anderson's owner hired an overseer during the Civil War who made immediate changes upon his arrival. "After dat, de hell start to pop, 'cause the first thing he do is cut rations. He weighs out de meat, three pound for the de weak, and he measure a peck of meal. And 'twarn't enough. He half starve us niggers and he want mo' work and he start the whippin's."[44] Wilson also commented that slave owners and overseers would often restrict the quantity of food available to those slaves that disobeyed.[45]

Often owners overlooked the brutal tactics of the overseers if it appeared that he had control and produced the desired amount of work. Henry Butler said he often heard the screams of slaves on the adjacent plantation. "One old slave called Jim, on the Rector place, disobeyed some rule and early one morning they ordered him to strip. They tied him to the whipping post and from morning until noon, at intervals, the lash was applied to his back."

Green Cumby

On large plantations it was not uncommon for a select few trusted black slaves to rise to the position of driver, which allowed them to manage other field slaves. Even when the professional overseer was present, there may have still been several drivers depending on the division of labor on the plantation. On smaller plantations, those without overseers, white slave owners depended heavily on the skill of the driver to manage other slaves, often as brutally as the overseer.[46]

In Texas, many former slaves indicated that they enjoyed special privileges because of someone in their family who held the position of driver. Green Cumby told his interviewer that his grandfather was the driver of forty slaves and had the responsibility of leading those slaves in the field. Cumby further said his grandfather frequently worked the other slaves from "sun to sun," and sometimes on Sundays. Likewise, Davis said his uncle was a driver who often punished fellow slaves for their lack of production.[47]

Surprisingly, black drivers often treated the slaves with more contempt than the white overseers.[48] Sarah Ford recalled the viciousness of the driver on the Kit Patton plantation, near West Columbia, Texas. This particular driver, known as Uncle Big Jake, was as black as any slave on the plantation but was also as mean and cruel as any white overseer. "He so mean I 'spect de devil done make him an overseer down below a long time ago." Ford blamed Patton for allowing Uncle Big Jake to punish the slaves so severely that many often ran away.[49]

There is no question that the master–slave relationship was perhaps *the* most contentious relationship in the antebellum South. Even though there were laws that protected the slave from the cruel excesses of the master, they appear to have been scarcely enforced as slave owners were free to treat their perceived chattel in any manner they chose. Slaves were well aware of their limitations and understood that any benevolence could be short-lived as their lives were at the mercy of someone else.

FOUR

THE PLANTATION'S LABOR

The role of the slave in Southern society was that of "beast of burden." Field slaves worked from before sunrise to past sunset. Those fortunate enough to serve the master in his house did not always fare much better. They served at the whim of the master and his family, and any indiscretion was met with severe punishments. Typically children worked around the house sweeping or running errands until they were old enough to move into the fields. Without question, slaves were expected to work and their memories of slave labor certainly influenced their memories of the master–slave relationship decades later.

In *From Slavery to Freedom*, historian John Hope Franklin made the argument that whites believed blacks were so lazy that they would not be productive without constant supervision and prodding. Therefore, the former slaves' perception of slavery and their former masters was closely related to their former work-related interactions with their masters, the hired overseer, or the driver.[1] For the majority of slaves, slavery meant back-breaking work because slavery was nothing more than a form of forced labor.[2]

Famed slave owner Willie Lynch once encouraged slave owners to use methods of control that would ensure maximum profitability from their slaves, which indicated the importance of slaves and their labor to the development of a regional economy based on agriculture. The methods of control described by Lynch were embraced by the Southern planters and became directly responsible for the adverse conditions that affected every fabric of the slave community, from work and the nature of the family to the ever-present threats of physical violence.[3]

Nonetheless, because slavery was a form of labor, the labor management of slaves consumed most of the energies of the master.[4] Because the profitability of

Clara Brim

the plantation rested on the productivity of its slaves, it was incumbent on the master to develop and implement a system, or combinations of systems, that would ensure productivity while maintaining the master–slave relationship.[5] Whites believed that most slaves cooperated with the plantation productivity through negative reinforcements such as the whip or forced family separations. Conversely, there were those whites that used positive reinforcements (e.g., such as extra rations) as a way to tie slaves to the land in the belief that it would lead to increased labor productivity. As a result, the two prevalent labor systems were known as the task and gang systems.[6]

The task system of work was one in which the slaves were assigned a specific amount of work that was to be completed within a specific amount of time. If slaves did not complete their assigned task within the specified time they would receive some form of punishment commensurate with the infraction. On the other hand, if the slave completed his or her assigned task before the specified time, he or she would enjoy some "personal" time with which they may work on their crops for their own benefit.[7]

Will Adams indicated that as slaves he and his family worked from "sun to sun" for Dave Cavin in Harrison County. However, Cavin allowed his slaves to grow their own crops, which they were allowed to cultivate on Saturdays. Cavin would buy the crops from his slaves and that allowed the slaves to have their own money, which was used to purchase clothes. "Lots saved money and bought freedom 'fore the war was over."[8]

Likewise, Clara Brim stated that as slaves they were also allowed to cultivate their own crops once their assigned work was complete. "When the slaves go to work, he give dem de task. Dat so much work, so many rows cotton to chop or corn to hoe. When dey git through dey can do what dey want. He task dem on Monday. Some dem git through Thursday night." This allowed the slaves three days to work their own crops, for which they received money, or they could hire themselves out on nearby plantations and earn extra wages that way.[9] Edgar Bendy also recollected being hired out to take care of white children. "I didn't do nothin' 'cept nuss babies. I jes jump them up and down and de old marster hire me out to nuss other white folks chillen, big and little."[10]

The task system allowed the slaves to enjoy a modicum of independence that those associated with the gang system did not. Still, the task system did not shorten the workday for most slaves.[11] The length of the workday was still dependent on the size of the plantation, the crops produced, and the temperament of the master. Some masters introduced the task system as a way of making slaves responsible for a particular field throughout the season's full cycle of ground preparation, planting, weeding, and ultimately harvesting. This was done to ensure the slaves felt a sense of responsibility for the productivity of that specific piece of land. They hoped that such responsibility might carry with it a sense of pride in doing a good job, which might in turn increase productivity through positive reinforcements.[12]

However, one of the inherent problems with the task system was that masters typically assigned tasks equally to the field hands. In this manner, the stronger field hands produced at the same level as the weaker field hands. This meant that the stronger field hands were not actually working to their full capacity. Also, in their eagerness to complete the assigned task and begin working for themselves, overseers reported an increase in careless work. Such carelessness led many masters to abandon the task system in favor of the gang system.[13]

There is enough evidence that suggests the gang system of labor was the most productive. Slaves worked in units supervised by an overseer or driver.[14] Each work group was assigned a specific responsibility in the full cycle of agricultural production, depending on the season of the year.[15] The overseer or the slave driver had the responsibility for ensuring the slaves were productive each day and typically worked the gang from the first break of daylight until exhaustion set in, sometimes ten to fourteen hours later. Although there was some consideration as to how much any particular gang could accomplish in a given day, the first consideration was productivity followed by the need to limit the amount of the slaves' free time.[16]

Austin Grant indicated that on the Harper plantation near Gonzales, the slaves worked all the time. "When you could see to work, you was workin' for him (the master)." They were not allowed to have their own gardens nor have any form of money for themselves. "He never paid anything, you never got to see none. Some of the Germans would give the old ones a little piece of money, but the chillen, pshaw! They never got to see nothin'."[17]

Sarah Ashley said that she worked in the fields picking cotton, "and sometimes pick 300 pound and tote it a mile to de cotton house. Some pick 300 to 800 pound cotton and have to tote de bag de whole mile to de gin." She also indicated there were consequences for not being as productive as the overseer believed you could be. "Iffen dedy didn't do dey work dey git whip till dey have blister on 'em."[18]

This supported the opinion among the masters that even when using these two forms of labor management to ensure and maintain plantation productivity, blacks were lazy and had to be driven hard to be productive. Eugene Genovese found this archaic attitude had less to do with black slavery and more to do with the racist European attitudes toward poor people. "When slaveholders insisted that blacks would work only long enough to provide for elementary and occasional debauchery, they were associating themselves with a theory generally held by English manufacturers, not to mention the clergy, about the laboring poor."[19]

Southern whites applied this European racist view of class not only as a means of ensuring production but also to justify the barbaric treatment of slaves. Whether out of fear or rewards, slaves did what was asked of them. However, it was naturally easier for slaves to work better for kind masters than those they considered cruel. Andy Anderson said he was never whipped by his first owner, but his second owner did not hesitate in using the whip to establish his sense of the master–slave relationship. As a result, Anderson indicated his level of work decreased. "After dat whippin' I doesn't have de heart to work for de massa. If I seed de cattle in de cornfield, I turns de back, 'stead of chasin' 'em out."[20] William Paxton said he experienced few whippings and stated "dere wasn't much whippin' only when de slaves was lazy." His recollection of slavery was based on his master's reaction to the slave's productivity. "Marse Paxton and de boys was mighty good to de slaves." This was based on the belief that the slaves on his plantation were productive and not perceived as being lazy.[21]

Ann Hawthorne said she was never whipped by her master and also believed that her master was good to his slaves. Such favorable memories of slavery were not based on what Hawthorne produced but rather on the fact that she said she never disobeyed. "Me? I never did git no lickin's when I was a li'l slave. No man. I allus did obey jis' like I was teached to do and dey didn't hafter whip me. I 'members dat."[22]

Regardless of the type of labor system implemented, the duties assigned to the plantation's slaves depended on the size of the plantation and the gender and age of the available labor (slaves). A majority of Texas slaves belonged to farmers owning at least ten slaves. On small plantations or farms little work specialization occurred. Slave females were typically responsible for those duties involving the upkeep of the house and the rearing of children. When necessary they worked in the fields alongside their husbands or other male members of the community. Slave males did whatever was necessary for the successful operation of the plantation. This meant the duties could be as varied as building fences to chopping wood to planting and harvesting crops.[23]

Tom Holland told how he chopped cotton, plowed the fields, and split rails when it was necessary, whereas Jerry Boykins said his father was a blacksmith and his mother was the cook. This allowed Boykins close contact in the big house where he remembered eating at the "white folks table, after dey done et." Children did as much work as they physically could. But at all times they were being instructed on the duties on that plantation and their future roles within the plantation world.[24]

On large plantations, those with twenty or more slaves, there might be separate tasks for men, women, children, domestic servants, the aged, and the typical field hand. If there was an overseer present, he usually directed the work of the field hands whereas the domestic, or house, slaves were generally directed by the mistress or a black slave that exerted increased responsibility and trust.[25]

The plantation was most often a self-contained unit requiring slaves to perform multiple tasks for to ensure profitable operations. Unfortunately, the various tasks led to a hierarchy of sorts within the slave community based on the complexion of the slaves. Records indicate that fairer-skinned slaves most often worked in and around the masters' houses and performed those tasks requiring some skill and expertise. Although field hands possessed the skill and knowledge to cultivate crops, they did not typically possess the same influence in the slave community when compared to house slaves.

Perhaps the most basic division of plantation labor was the separation of the house slave and the field slave.[26] Although there is a slight differentiation between *servant* and *slave*, in the plantation context any attempt to place more status and respect on the servant label is an exercise in academic futility. Even though they may have enjoyed a few more privileges than their field counterparts, house slaves understood that they were nonetheless slaves. Black females were more often found in occupations in and around the main house.[27] They became the responsibility of the plantation mistress and maintained the cleanliness of the master's house, performed the cooking duties, sewed clothes, and did the washing and ironing. In those instances when slave men were kept around the main house, they usually functioned as butlers and yardmen.[28]

Although many slave females worked in the fields, there were still others that performed a variety of duties in and around the big house. Francis Black was a house girl who washed and ironed clothes.[29] Fannie Brown worked as a seamstress. However, her training as a seamstress was not without its punishments. "Missy larnt me to spin and weave and did dis child git many a whippin' 'fore I could do it good. Den she larnt me to cook and start me cookin' two or three days 'fore company come."[30]

Even though as a child she was too young to work, Josie Brown remembered that her mother was also a seamstress but had the additional responsibility of being a wet nurse to her thirteen children plus the master's seven. Kate Darling and Mary Kincheon Edwards also wet-nursed their master's children. However, Darling said she also worked in the fields where they lived in constant fear of the lash. "He'd whip the man for half doin' the plowin' or hoein' but if they done it right, he'd find something else to whip them for."[31]

Edwards said in addition to being the wet nurse she was also the seamstress, and, depending on the season, she worked in the field. "De most work I done for de Vaughns was wet nuss de baby son, what name Elijah. His mamy jes didn't have 'nough milk for him." She continued, "I didn't mind pickin' cotton, 'cause I never did have de backache. I pick two and three hunnert pounds a day and one day I picked four hunnert."[32]

Millie Forward said she was born in Alabama, but when her master, Jason Forward, moved the family and his slaves to Texas near Jasper, she was separated from her father because he lived on another plantation. As a result, the Forwards treated her and her siblings "jes like dey us pappy and mammy." She spent the remainder of slavery as a housegirl serving the women of the master's family.[33]

Trusted house slaves often functioned as surrogate plantation managers in the absence of the master and his family. John Boles found that the slave masters and the plantation mistresses often grew so dependent on the skills of the house slave that the house slave could sometimes manipulate them for their benefit. "Life in the big house was a never ending process of give and take, and masters sometimes found themselves psychologically almost as enslaved to the system as were blacks."[34] But rarely did the house slave develop any pretensions of status above the rest of the slave community. Even the mammy, who typically had free access throughout the main house, was not in a position to consider herself "different." They all understood that they were first and foremost slaves, and the master controlled every aspect of their lives.

Many times children were brought to the main house as the personal slave to the master's children. Although this may seem to be a better condition than field work, it often led to the disruption of the slave family who soon found themselves unable to control to maintain family and cultural ties with that child. This also led to the disintegration of the slave community because of the conflict that ensued between the house slaves and the field slaves. There were times when the house slave began to identify and assume the mannerism of the master's family versus that of the slave community. Some field slaves even considered the house slaves as spies for the master.[35] As a child, William Adams worked around the house running errands and serving his mistress. He commented that it was his responsibility to light her pipe and help her knit.[36] Stearlin Arnwine also indicated that he enjoyed slave life as a child because his duties as a houseboy. His primary responsibility was that of taking his master's children to school on Mondays and retrieving them on Fridays.[37]

House slaves enjoyed more frequent contact with whites than field slaves and experienced the best, and sometimes, the worst conditions of slavery. Many of the house slaves received a level of respect among the slave community because of their proximity to the big house and the master. Ellen Betts recalled how her Aunt Rachel was not only respected by the master's family but also by the slave community as well. "All de niggers have to stoop to Aunt Rachel jes' like dey curtsey to Missy."[38] Even though house slaves enjoyed the advantages of better food, clothing, and housing, their work schedule still depended upon the needs of the master and the master's family. This led to irregular working hours with little time for leisure or personal work pursuits. Harriett Barrett remembered her mother working as a cook for the master's family during the day, but at night he locked up the slaves to prevent them from running away. "Massa, he have big bunch slaves and work dem long as dey could see and den lock 'em up in de quarters at night to keep 'em from runnin' off."[39] Additionally, house slaves were also under the direct scrutiny of the master and every infraction, no matter how small, was possibly a punishable offense.

Many ex-slaves even remembered living in the big house and not the slave quarters. This was generally reserved for those slaves with the responsibility of serving the master's children or who were themselves children of the master. Callie Shepard, born in 1852, slept in the big house and described her owner, Master Stevens, as a, "right livin' man and dey allus good to me and my mammy." Her "mammy" was a "little red-Indian nigger woman," and they knew they received better treatment than Stevens's other slaves. Shepard understood that many slaves were not as fortunate as they were and commented on how the other slaves were treated. "I seed 'em whip de niggers 'cause dey tolt the chillen to look. Dey buckled 'em down on de groun' and laid it on de backs. Sometimes dey laid on with a mighty heavy hand. But I ain't never git no whippin' 'cause I never went with de cullud gen'ration. I set right in de buggy with de white chillen."[40]

Albert Todd and Emma Watson were house slaves with the responsibility of caring for the master's children. Todd's sole responsibility was the protection of the slave owner's daughter to and from school.[41] Watson, who did not specifically state what her responsibilities were relative to the children, merely stated that she cared for the master's many children.[43]

Victor Duhon recalled his mother being a house slave and the concubine to the master's son, whom he believed to be his father. As a result, Duhon said he had his own room in the big house. "You know, Madame Duhon was my grandma. She was good to me." Because of his parentage, Duhon never felt a part of the larger slave community. "I didn't play much with the black children. My time went waiting on my white folks."[43]

Cato Carter's father was also white, and like Victor Duhon, enjoyed the privileges of having his own room in the big house. "I had a room built on the big house, where I stayed, and they was allus good to me, 'cause I's one of their blood."[44] Even though he enjoyed the benefit of living in close proximity to whites, Carter was still apprehensive during his interview and indicated there were some aspects of slavery he could not reveal.

Emma Watson

Like Carter and Duhon, Thomas Cole also told of sharing a room in the big house with his mother, sister, and brother. He also remembered eating at the table after the master's family finished their meals. Still, he commented that the lives of the other slaves were not like those of his family. Cole said his master worked the field slaves like "mules."[45]

However, the majority of slaves were classified as field hands. Although men and women were found in the fields, especially during the harvest time, these outside tasks were generally reserved to men.[46] Still, there were women, like Clara Brim, who not only worked in the fields but also outproduced most men.[47] Likewise, Annie Osborne remembered her mother working in the fields along side the other men. "My mammy plowed and hoed and chopped and picked cotton and jus' as good as the menfolks."[48] On a typically plantation 60 percent of the slave community had to be available to work in the fields. The remaining 40 percent generally represented children and the aged.[49]

There were numerous jobs performed by field hands. Because crop labor varied depending on the time of year, field hands might also work at clearing land, cutting firewood, and repairing barns and fences. On the large plantations, there were definite skilled jobs that required special training. In addition to working in the fields, some slaves were also trained as craftsmen, including blacksmiths, bricklayers, carpenters, whereas the most trusted slave might find himself charged with being the slave driver. The driver, black or white, was directly responsible for the slaves' day-to-day productivity.

Field hands on cotton plantations usually prepared the ground during the nongrowing season by turning the ground with a hoe or ax. At harvest time, the typical field slave might be expected to pick at least ninety pounds of cotton per day. Rice cultivation required an intensive amount of labor and supervision. Typically, rice plantations had more slaves per acre than tobacco or cotton plantations. Work on these plantations was usually accomplished by the task system, which allowed the slave to complete a certain amount of work per day. The advantage to the slave was that if he or she worked diligently there would be time left in the day to work for his or her own purposes. The annual cycle of rice cultivation began in December or January when the fields were prepared for the spring planting, which began in March or April. Harvesting began in late summer and continued until November or December when the process started over again. On sugar plantations, the planting season occurred from January through the spring and was also labor intensive.[50]

Both Harrison Boyd and Gus Bradshaw worked as field hands. Boyd said on his plantation they grew a variety of crops that included peas, pumpkins, corn, and cotton.[51] Bradshaw indicated the primary crop on his plantation was cotton. He indicated that everyone, young or old, male or female, picked cotton.[52] Likewise, Mattie Gilmore confirmed that on most cotton plantations, everyone was involved in one way or another in the cultivation of cotton. However, sometimes working in the fields became a dangerous pursuit, especially for women with newborn babies. "Some de women what had suckin' babies left dem in de shade while they worked, and one time a big bald eagle flew down by one dem babies and picked it up and flew away with it. De mama couldn't git it and we never heard of dat baby 'gain."[53]

Perhaps the most common image of slavery is that of the slave laboring in the cotton fields. Although there may have been some debate as to slavery's continued profitability by the onset of the Civil War in Texas and throughout the South, slave labor was definitely a vital component of the Texas economy at emancipation. Regardless of the methods used by the slave owner in managing his slaves, the slave was expected to produce.

On larger plantations, slave owners had the luxury of assigning slaves to specific duties. It has always been assumed that the division of slaves based on skin tone was a contentious issue on the plantation. However, there is little evidence that suggests there were any real conflicts between the house and the field slaves. Because divisions of labor was only possible on large plantations, and even then, it was not unusual for those assigned to the house to help in the fields.[54] Therefore, any pretended division was generally temporary and short-lived. Certainly, there were those plantations that resembled those described in the novel *Gone with the Wind*, but those assigned to the house also understood that their condition was generally no better than those laboring in the fields, because at the end of the day, they were both still slaves.

FIVE

FIGHT THE POWER

Although the slave toiling away in the cotton fields is perhaps the most recognizable image of slavery, the image of the runaway slave carries another connotation of desperation and the desire to be free at all costs, even if that cost was ones' life. Volumes have been written about Harriet Tubman and the activities of the Underground Railroad leading blacks out of slavery and into freedom. Many of the ex-slaves interviewed in Texas discussed in detail their personal knowledge of those who attempted to run away and why. Escape was only one form used by slaves to fight the power and control of their masters and overseers. Black slaves were also known to physically confront whites and destroy property. Many of these attempts were futile and often resulted in severe punishments or death.

However, the images of the desperate slave are contrary to that of Elkins' docile Sambo. Such contradictions bring into question why slaves were seen as lazy and shiftless on one hand, but capable of extreme violence on the other. The narratives indicate that slaves routinely fought against their forced enslavement when they could, but pacified whites with seemingly "good" behavior at other times. As a result, the Southern perspective of slavery recalled the slave as being dependent upon white generosity, even though the former slaves often commented on their willingness to risk everything to be free.[1]

Jim Crow America willingly embraced this stereotype of blacks, even though it was manufactured by whites who continued defending slavery, and its so-called paternalism, as being necessary because blacks were incapable of managing themselves in a civilized society. However, the former slaves in Texas illustrated that their often perceived docility was in fact a ruse designed

Mary Armstrong

to manipulate white slave owners for *their* benefit. They also described numerous instances in which black slaves fought against the brutal nature of slavery, sometimes at a cost of their own lives.

Many of Texas' former slaves said they physically fought back against the control exerted by their former masters and overseers and many even conspired to destroy property. Mary Armstrong remembered hitting her mistress in the eye with a rock because the mistress was responsible for the death of Armstrong's baby sister. "[A]nd I picks up a rock 'bout as big as half your fist and hits her right in the eye and busted the eyeball, and tells her that's for whippin' my baby sister to death. You could her holler for five miles."[2]

Jacob Branch also recalled a physical confrontation with his master's wife, who wanted to whip him because she believed he was "gittin' it too good, 'cause he aint never been whipped." Branch said one day she climbed over a fence and approached him with a leather cow whip. He stopped where he was and raised the hoe he was working with high in the air and said defiantly, "Missy, I ain't 'vise you to come any step closeter." He said she heeded his warning.[3]

Ex-slave William Hamilton conveyed to his interviewer that he knew of a woman, Jane Bensom, who fought against the authority of the "Ku Klux" before emancipation. Even though Hamilton recalled the white racist group as being part of the infamous Ku Klux Klan, it is unlikely that they were because the Klan did not officially appear until after 1865. Nonetheless, his recollection of bands of whites roaming the countryside randomly attacking blacks should not be discounted because these individuals most likely became a part of the Klan once they arrived in Texas. Regardless, Hamilton indicated that these groups of whites routinely beat slaves after dark without justification. "It am allus after dark when dey comes to de house and catches de man and whups him for nuthin'. Dey has de power, and it am done for to show dey has de power." However, one day Bensom, who Hamilton described as "lots of woman, wide as de door and tall, and weighs 'bout three hunder pounds," gathered embers from the fireplace and waited until the "Klux" burst through her door. She then threw the embers in their faces and quickly escaped out the back door. "Two of dem am burnt purty bad. . . . De nex' night back dey comes and asks where Jane am. She 'longs to Massa John Ditto and am so big everybody knows her, but de niggers won't tell on her. She leaves de country fin'ly, but dey comes lookin' for her every night for two months."

Slaves on the Timmins Plantation, located in east Texas, confessed to a plot to poison their owners and then physically destroy the plantation. Other slaves throughout the region were aware of the plot, and some tried to discourage this uprising. Eventually, the plot was discovered, but when the slaves involved were questioned, they indicated that they were coerced by an unidentified white man to harm their master and his family.[4] Unfortunately, no other information was given as to the motives of this "unknown white male." In fact, it is entirely possible that he did not exist and was merely an attempt by the slaves to create an alibi. It is also entirely possible that these slaves were aware of the paranoia that existed among slaveholders that Northern white abolitionist were instigating black slaves to murder their owners.

Although the plot on the Timmins Plantation failed, there were many other violent acts committed by slaves that were successful. Slave owner William Gaffeney was killed by two of his own slaves, later identified as John and Mose. After their capture, it did not take a jury long to find the pair guilty. After the verdict, observers noticed the attitude and demeanor of John and Mose was one of "stoic indifference."[5] Two weeks later, the gathered crowd cheered as they were hanged.[6] In another case, Jane Elkins, a female slave, became the first person hanged in Dallas County in 1853. The facts were unclear as to the events that led to the death of her owner, but she was nonetheless convicted of his murder and sentenced to death.[7]

In an unusual instance of violence committed by slaves, a local newspaper told a story of deception, murder, and vigilante retribution. Two slaves belonging to a Mr. Dales of Washington County lured his neighbor Mr. Fisk to his death. Pretending Mr. Dales's child was sick, the pair convinced Mr. Fisk, apparently a physician, to leave his house to give aid to the child. Once outside the safety of his home, Dales's slaves "knocked him in the head with an axe and killed him." Next, they proceeded to the Fisk's home and "one of them knocked down Mrs. Fisk with his fists and after brutally accomplishing their desires on her, killed her with the same axe that killed her husband." The pair then murdered the Fisk's child and set the house on fire "in two places and left." There was no indication how the two slaves were eventually captured, but local residents believed it was necessary to make an example of them in hopes of deterring similar behaviors in the county's numerous slaves; vigilantes lynched and burned them.[8]

Local newspapers frequently reported acts of violence committed by slaves against their owners. This indicates that the black slaves in Texas did not all see the master–slave relationship as genially paternalistic. In fact, Texas' slaves may have been closer in behavior to the firebrand Nat Turner than to Elkin's submissive Sambo. For example, the *Texas State Gazette* reported the death of James Gentry at the hands of two of his slaves, a male and a female. According to the article, the male knocked Gentry down with an axe, and the "Negro woman completed the murder." The two then burned his body to conceal the murderous act. However, neighbors noticed Gentry's absence, searched his plantation, and came across a smoldering heap, a few bones, and "some brass buttons." The pair eventually confessed. At this point, observers described them as having "a very bad countenance, their appearance is brutal and revolting."[9]

Even though the opportunity to physical confront the slave owner existed, in general, slaves chose other paths of resistance. Slave owners often worried about the movements of slaves throughout the region, in particular runaway slaves. Runaways not only meant a loss of resources (when one considers slaves as resources) but also the potential that productivity might suffer because of the diminished available labor. To deter slaves from running away from the plantation, slaveholders developed and encouraged regional slave patrols. These white males, often described by the former slaves as "pore white trash," patrolled the streets and had the unofficial authority to question, and sometimes punish, any slave they encountered travelling between plantations.[10] Their general objective was the control of the black community through physical intimidation.[11]

Furthermore, historians Kenneth Stampp and Sally Hadden found the patrollers to be closely associated with the militia, which meant their activities, as a pseudo-police force were sanctioned by local legislatures.[12] Acting as law enforcement, slave owners looked to the patrollers to keep an eye on potential rebellions and either prevent them before they occurred or notify the owners of potential uprising, thus allowing the owners to inflict whatever punishments they deemed appropriate.

Local Texas officials became extremely concerned about the numbers of runaways escaping to Mexico. By 1844, local newspapers encouraged anyone finding runaway slaves west of San Antonio to collect a reward of fifty dollars when they returned the slaves to their rightful owner. Two years later, the state legislature directed local county courts to create a formal patrol designed to guard specific districts periodically with the power to search slaves and property.[13]

It did not matter if the slaves were near San Antonio or Lynchburg, Virginia, the slave patrols liberally punished any slave unable to present a pass that allowed them to be away from their respective plantations.[14] This further illustrates the continuity of slavery in Texas with the remainder of the Confederacy. Nonetheless, the threats of punishments were not enough to prevent some slaves from slipping away without a pass. Tom Holland recalled how he was caught by the patrols, who he called "patterrollers."

> If we went off without a pass we allus went two at a time. We slipped off when we got a chance to see young folks on some other place. The patterrollers cotched me one night and, Lawd have mercy me, they stretches me over a log and hits thirty-nine licks with a rawhide loaded with rock, and every time they hit me the blood and hide done fly.[15]

Holland continued by saying he was unable to work for days after the beating. Still, he continued to fight against the rules by leaving without a pass. So for Holland, no amount of whippings or other punishments would deter him from challenging the authority of the patrols.

The master–slave relationship was a tenuous one at best. The indoctrination and forced acceptance of slavery occurred early in childhood and few openly challenged the authority of those who held the whip. Whether it was the master, overseer, or another slave acting as the driver, the slaves understood their role in slavery, which was complete submission to white authority. Some dared challenge white authority, often choosing pain instead of compliance. Even though white authority most often manifested itself in the work of the slaves, it was nonetheless obvious in their day-to-day existence.

Even with the known examples of rebellions and physical confrontations throughout the South, the most common form of resistance involved attempts to escape the plantation and the control of the master and overseer.[16] Slaves would run collectively and singularly, depending on the opportunity and their familial ties. Another influence in the decision to escape was the location of the plantation and the surrounding geography. Slaves would often seek refuge in nearby wooded areas, swamps, and mountainous regions when available, until it was determined that they could proceed further.[17] For example, Jenny Proctor, Cato Carter, and Julia Blanks indicated that many so-called runaway slaves actually hid out in the nearby woods and would often be assisted by other slaves who would give them food and clothes.[18]

In his discussion of runaways in Texas, Rupert Richardson commented that "Those in bondage longed for freedom."[19] Randolph Campbell agreed with this assessment when he said that Texas' slaves often ran away. He also added that the motivation was to either reunite with displaced family or merely to escape the brutality of slavery. However, unlike other regions of the South, blacks in Texas not only sought freedom by running north, but also south across the Rio Grande to Mexico.[20]

Many Texas slaves looked south across the Rio Grande for true escape, and they were often aided by local Mexicans. The *Houston Telegraph* and *Texas Ranger* reported twenty-five slaves ran away from a Bastrop plantation. The escape was facilitated by a group of unknown Mexicans and all were seen headed toward the Rio Grande. The implication was that the runaways and their facilitators may have been destined for a Mexican settlement just south of the Rio Grande.[21] Likewise, local officials in Goliad also accused a local Mexican laborer of stealing the slave of A. H. Bisco. Eventually, the slave was captured and returned to his owner. For his trouble, the "thief" received "150 lashes on his bare back and the letter 'T' branded on his forehead."[22]

Texas slave owners always understood the problems associated with slaves escaping into Mexico. Even before Sam Houston's victory at San

Jacinto, many slave owners were concerned about the possibility of General Antonio Lopez de Santa Anna's army inciting the slaves to cooperate with their efforts to defeat the defiant Texians.[23] Likewise, there were concerns about the purchase of some slave because of the possibility that he or she might try to escape to Mexico.[24]

Once a slave crossed the Rio Grande into Mexico he or she was generally accepted by Mexicans. Once fluent in Spanish, ex-slaves easily assimilated into Mexican culture and society. Frederick Law Olmstead commented that slaves desired freedom in any manner possible, and the escape to Mexico was one way of illustrating the lengths that they went through to escape the brutality of slavery.[25] For example, Felix Haywood said even though individuals, presumably whites, would encourage the slaves to run north, he believed heading south was a better option. "We used to laugh at that. There wasn't no reason to run up North. All we had to do was walk, but walk South, and we'd bee [sic] free as soon as we crossed the Rio Grande. . . . In Mexico you could be free. They didn't care what color you was, black, white, yellow or blue. Hundreds of slaves did go to Mexico and got all right. We would hear about 'em and how they was goin' to be Mexicans. They brought up their children to speak only Mexican."[26]

Jacob Branch also remembered Texas slaves escaping south into Mexico during the Civil War. "All dem in dis part heads for de Rio Grande river. De Mexicans rig up flatboats out in de middle de river, tied to stakes with ropes. When de cullud people gits to de rope dey can pull deyself 'cross de reat de way on dem boats. De white folks red de Mexican side dat river all de time, but plenty slaves git through, anyway."[27]

To discourage runaways, Texas slave owners used punishments and often enlisted the help of the white community in reclaiming runaway slaves through such means as personal correspondence or the local newspapers. Former slaves William Adams and Harriet Barrett remembered slave owners using dogs to track down runaway slaves. When the slaves were captured, as they most often were, their punishments ranged from whippings to being chained and locked up during the day and night.[28]

Ex-slave Thomas Cole told his WPA interviewer that when he was a slave in Alabama, he escaped and headed north hoping to meet up with Harriet Tubman, who he believed would help him the rest of the way to freedom. Instead, he was discovered by Union soldiers and eventually forced into service in the Union Army.

> I crosses de river and goes north. I's gwine to de free country, where dey ain't no slaves. I travels all dat day and night up de river and follows de north star. Sev'ral times I think de blood hou's am trailin' me and I gits in de big hurry. I's so tired I couldn't hardly move, but I gits in a trot.
>
> I's hopin' and prayin' all de time meets up with dat Harriet Tubman woman. She de cullud woman what takes slaves to Canada. She allus travels de underground railroad, dey calls it, travels at night and hides out in de day. She sho' sneaks dem out de South and I thinks she's a brave woman.
>
> I eats all de nuts and kills a few swamp rabbits and cotches a few fish. I builds de fire and goes off 'bout half a mile and hides in de thicket till it burns down to de coals, den bakes me some fish and rabbit. I's shakin' all de time. 'fraid I'd git cotched, but I's nearly starve to death. I puts de rest de fish in my cap and travels on dat night by de north star and hides in a big thicket de nex' day and along evenin' I hears guns shootin'. I sho' am scart dis time, sho' 'nough. I's scart to come in and scart to go out, and while I's standin' dere, I hears two men say. 'Stick you hands up, boy. What you doin'?' I says, 'Uh-uh-uh, I dunno. You ain't gwine take me back to de plantation, is you?' Dey says, 'No. Does you want to fight for de North?' I says I will.[29]

Help from the local community was also a way of maintaining control and discouraging slaves from trying to escape. A planter from Victoria sought the help of a neighbor in finding a slave who apparently made a habit of escaping because he said he was looking for "my Negro man Bill who left again on Saturday night."[30]

Slave owners in Texas were especially disturbed by the loss of their skilled slaves and would offer huge sums in reward money for their capture and safe return. In his plantation journal, Julian Devereux made a notation to make inquiries for an escaped slave on behalf of another slave owner. Incidentally, the slave owner posted a reward of fifty dollars for the runaway.[31]

The *Texas Ranger* newspaper described the theft of a forty-five-year-old slave, supposedly "stolen" by a white male. The slave's owner, E. L. Arnold described his property as "a Negro boy named Hector, 45 years old, hair somewhat gray, and is a tolerably good rough carpenter." The article further advertised a reward of fifty dollars for the "recovery of the boy," and another one hundred dollars for the "arrest of the white man" allegedly responsible for the theft.[32]

John Random offered two hundred dollars for the return of two male runaway slaves. Instead of providing generic descriptions, Random provided detailed physical information about his two slaves, Will and Adam. Random described Will as being between thirty-one or thirty-two years old, very black with a small scar on his forehead. Adam was younger, twenty-four or twenty-five years old, with half of his forefinger on his left hand missing. In addition to the missing finger, Random said Adam was "inclined to be yellow, looks sour."[33]

Edwin Waller used the local paper to offer a reward of two hundred dollars for "two African Negroes, named Gumby and Zaw" that escaped from his Brazoria County plantation. The physical description included the usual height and weight of each slave, in addition to observing that one of the runaways had a "wild look."[34] James Rogers of Gilmer offered a "liberal reward" for the return of two male runaways. One of the slaves was said to have a "downcast look when closely questioned," and the other "a very hobbling, rocking kind of walk." He not only wanted his slaves returned, but the mules they used to make their escape.[35]

Although slave owners offered most of the rewards personally, there were several instances in which a third party was involved. C. W. Buckley advertised in both the *Houston Telegraph* and the *Texas Ranger* a reward for the capture and return of a female runaway. The papers described the slave as a "Negro woman named Emily, about 25 years of age, dark complexion, medium height and rather fleshy." The ad was listed on behalf of the slave's owner, Thomas Gardner.[36] Likewise, $150 dollars was offered by A. J. Austin on behalf of A. Bryan for the return of his slave, a "mulatto man named Ned, about 26 years old, and his wife, a black woman named Darcus or Rose, about 28 years old."[37]

Sometimes the civil authorities also participated in the capture of runaway slaves. The sheriff of Travis County recorded the capture of a runaway he described as "riding a small Bay pony and wearing a straw hat and decently clothed."[38] What was particularly interesting about the involvement of civil authorities in the capture of slaves was the bill typically sent to the slave owner for the housing of runaways until repossession could take place. In the preceding instance involving the Travis County sheriff, a bill was sent to the owner for $18.25, which included $3.25 for the care of the horse and only $3.00 for the care of the runaway slave.[39]

Still, the vastness and sparse settlement in many regions throughout Texas made it difficult to reclaim runaway slaves. This sparseness also made Texas a popular destination for runaways from other slave states. The *Texas Ranger* reported that a man from "another state" advertised in several Texas newspapers asking for help in finding a "Negro fellow named Clayborn, aged 33. Said Negro is a mulatto, weighs about 150 pounds, rather stout built, about 5 feet 7 or 8 inches, speaks quick and is a blacksmith by trade." However, the paper cautioned readers that it might be difficult to find this runaway because "he will not easily disclose the name of his owner." The slave owner concluded his plea for help by offering a "liberal" reward to anyone with valid information about his "missing property."[40]

When slaves were captured, the punishments were often brutal. In his epic journey through Texas, Olmstead described a slave owner that drove a pitchfork into the face of a runaway hiding in a hayloft.[41] In another instance Olmstead described how a slave who was allowed to hire out his labor refused to work again for his owner. After being threatened with the whip by the owner, the slave responded by attacking his master and the master's son with a knife before fleeing. Olmstead did not indicate if the slave was captured or not, but noted that those in search of him commented that his actions belied the gentle paternalism of his master and that such treatment would likely change when he was returned.[42]

It was this fear of reprisal that led many slaves to understand that escape meant either freedom or death. A white slave owner identified as Latt reported that two of his slaves not only escaped, but also took two of his best horses. He believed they were headed south to Mexico and alerted officials near the border. US soldiers stationed near Brownsville intercepted the pair and ordered them to surrender. However, the slaves refused to obey their commands and were subsequently shot and killed. The Texas Ranger reported the incident and said, "The killing of the Negroes has been a serious loss to Mr. Latt as they were two of his most valuable hands."[43]

Although most records indicated the slave's willingness to risk his or her life in escape attempts, life as a fugitive was not guaranteed to be better than that of a slave. Runaways were suddenly forced to find their own shelter and food and survive in a world in which the color of their skin automatically placed them in a distinct caste structure in which they had no legal or civil rights. Ex-slave Marshall Showers remembered the safety and security of plantation life when he said "I like de old times best. Den I has plenty to eat and good clothes and' a good time."[44] Yet Kenneth Stampp found that slaves continually assumed the risks if it meant even the slightest possibility of freedom.[45] Lastly, there is sufficient evidence that indicates Stanley Elkins's docile Sambo might not have really existed given the more than two hundred incidents of revolts and conspiracies.[46]

The experiences of slaves in Texas illustrate the continuity with existing literature concerning the antebellum relationship between slave and master. Slaves were expected to completely submit to the will of their owner. As such, the plantation environment was often violent and brutal. Whether it was the master, overseer, driver, patrols, or the Ku Klux Klan, the plantation system reinforced the notion that blacks were ideally at the lower end of the societal ladder. However, many slaves did try to take some control of their lives through physical retaliation or running away. Given the proximity of Texas to Mexico, many masters were overly concerned about runaways. Nevertheless, blacks as a whole were unable to escape their perceived place at the bottom of white society's caste system, an expectation that did not easily go away, even during the early years of the twentieth century.

SIX

THE SLAVE FAMILY

The nature of the black family, in particular the black male-female relationship, is perhaps the most discussed subject in the black community today. Issues, such as HIV/AIDS and "down low brothers," continue to resonate through the black community and impacts the ways black men and women interact with one another. In antebellum Texas, black women sometimes had little say in who would be their "babies' daddy." In fact, black men were often used as breeders and encouraged to father as many children as possible. Of course there was an economic principle behind this because slave children could be sold as one might sell cattle or other livestock. However, the social implications were, and *are*, frightening. Black men were often not allowed to know their children or have any input in their rearing. Even in those situations in which the black family seemed stable, everyone knew and understood that the family could be torn part at the whim of the master.

Historian Peter Kolchin found that slave marriages were probably the slave's best mechanism in surviving slavery. He also argued that such unions, when permitted, were resilient during slavery and often endured beyond emancipation.[1] Other studies often found that black slaves mimicked the lifestyles of their white owners in the way in which they formally celebrated their wedding ceremonies. When such festivities were allowed by the slave owners, slave marriage ceremonies might consist of the slave owner reading a few passages from the Bible or the act of jumping over the broom. Often, slave owners encouraged slave marriages, voluntary and involuntary, because they believed married slaves caused fewer disciplinary problems because of the threat of separations. Even when encouraged, slave marriages were not legally binding in white society because slave owners still considered slaves, married or not, property.[2]

However, the former slaves indicated to their WPA interviewers that despite their best efforts to create some semblance of family, they sometimes had little choice in when, or whom, they would marry, and they also indicated that they successfully established stable patriarchal families in which marriages were an important element in the slave community. As such, fathers were often respected members of the slave community and the mothers typically shared common duties, for example, the raising of children, cooking, and cleaning.[3] The slave community also established its own guidelines for the sexual interactions of its members. In his study of the black family, historian Herbert Gutman found that slaves often frowned upon adultery and overt fornication. "For at least a quarter century prior to the Civil War, the Beaufort Baptist Church, most if not all of its members South Carolina slaves, punished people guilty of adultery and fornication. To commit adultery meant suspension from the church for three months."[4]

Still, many slaves in Texas were not allowed to marry. For example, ex-slave John Barker said, "Dey wan't 'lowed to marry, 'cause they could be sold and it wasn't no use, but you could live with 'em."[5] Still, other former slaves recalled choosing their own mates and discussed their wedding ceremonies and slave marriages. Although these ceremonies were not legal in the sense of being recognized by the county or state, they nonetheless were respected on the plantations. Slave weddings often involved dancing, food, and the act of jumping the broom and were considered big events in the slave community.

Ex-slave Phoebe Henderson recalled the big celebrations on the Hill plantation whenever slaves married. "When a couple marry, the master give them a house and we had a good time and plenty to wear and eat." The narrative suggests the interviewer asked her if her wedding to David Henderson was involuntary, to which she replied, "No, suh, Master Hill didn't have nothin' to do with bringin' us together. I guess God done it. We fell in love, and David asked Master Hill for me. We had a weddin' in the house and was married by a colored Baptist preacher. I wore a white cotton dress and Missus Hill give me a pan of flour for a weddin' present. He give us a house of our own."[6]

In her recollections of slave marriages, ex-slave Lucinda Elder commented that they were often informal relationships. "Dem days dey don't marry by no license. Dey takes a slave man and woman from de same plantation and puts 'em together, or sometime a man from 'nother plantation, like mama and papa."[7] However, Elder also remembered how their owner threw a big party whenever slaves got married. "Mama say Marse John give 'em a big supper in de big house and read out de Bible 'bout obeyin' and workin' and den dey am married. Course, de nigger jes a slave and have to do what de white folks say, so dat way of marryin' 'bout good as any."[8]

Ex-slave John Ellis from San Angelo said "I nev'r hear tell of many colored weddin's. We jes' jumps over de broom an' de bride she has to jump over it backwards and iffen she couldn' jump it backward she couldn't git married. Dat was sho' funny, seein' dem colored gi'ls a tryin' to jump dat broom."[9]

Interviewed in Houston, ex-slave Van Moore told his interviewer how his parents came to be married, even though they had separate owners.

> My mammy's name was Mary Moore and my pappy's name was Tom Moore. Mammy 'longed to the Cunninghams by Pappy 'longed to de McKinneys, what was Missy Cunningham's sister and her husban'. That's how my mammy and pappy come together. . . . In dem days a slave man see a slave gal what he wants and he asks his old massa, kin he see her. Iffen she owned by someone else, de massa ask de gal's massa iffen it all right to put 'em together and iffen he say so, dey jus' did. Twa'nt no Bible weddin', like now.[10]

Joe Barnes and Fred Brown remembered slave weddings as being the simple formality of jumping the broom. Barnes said, "Massa marry de folks in de broomstick style. Us don' have de party but sometime us sing and play games, like de round dance."[11] Brown also commented that when slave couples were allowed to get married, "De couple steps over de broom on de floor, dey's married den."[12]

However, former slaves Betty Powers and Tom Holland recalled slave marriages that were little more than arrangements. Powers said that as far as she recalled, slaves did not have weddings and that they were just "put together. . . . White man, you knows better'n dat. Dem times, cullud folks jus' put together. De massa say, 'Jim and Nancy, you go live together,' and when dat order give, it better be done. Dey thinks nothin' on de plantation 'bout de feelin's of de women and dere ain't no' spect for dem."[13]

Holland of Madisonville confirmed that in his narrative that slave marriage ceremonies were not elaborate affairs. "I asks misses if I could have Imogene and she says yes and that's all they was to our weddin'. . . . My weddin' clothes was a white loyal shirt, never had no shoes, married barefooted."[14] Holland nonetheless commented that the relationship lasted beyond slavery and produced three boys and three girls.

Sadly, slaves had little control over whom they would marry, when they would marry, or the number of children they would have.[15] Although there were instances of slave marriages extending beyond emancipation, there were also numerous examples that illustrated that stable, voluntary slave relationships were difficult to maintain. The possibility of a slave female finding a mate was impacted by numerous factors, such as the plantation's size, existing familial relationships, and the desires of the slave owners. As a result, many slave females had few choices in mate selection, and often the slave owner chose their mates for them.[16]

For example, former slave William Mathews from Galveston remembered that the some of the slaves were free to choose their own mates, but they had no control over their families because the slave owners could always decide who would remain married and who would not. "A gal go out and take de notion for some buck and dey make de 'greement to live together." He said that sometimes the slave owner could separate any couple when it suited him; "If a unhealthy buck take up with a portly gal, de white folks sep'rate 'em. If a man a big, stout man, good breed, dey gives him four, five women."[17]

Ex-slave Katie Darling's memories of slave marriages also mentioned that the wishes of the slave were of little concern to their former masters. In her opinion, the objective of marriages during "bullwhip days" was the rearing of as many children as possible. "Niggers didn't cou't then like they do now, massa pick out a po'tly man and a po'tly gal and jist put 'em together. What he want am stock."

Like Darling's narrative, ex-slave Lulu Wilson's remembrances of slavery also confirmed that her former owner, Wash Hodges, cared little about the feelings of his slaves. She said her father was a free black, but he was allowed to live on the plantation to be with her and her mother. However, she was the only child born to this union, and she believed Hodges expected her mother to have more children. "They say my paw am too old and wore out for breedin' and wants her to take with this here young buck." Hodges had the hound run off her father and put her mother with this "young buck. . . . So she took with my step-paw and they must of pleased the white folks what wanted niggers to breed like livestock, 'cause she birthed nineteen chillen."[18]

Former slave Thomas Johns from Cleburne also witnessed slave owners manipulating the intimate relationships of slaves. Johns said it was not uncommon for slave owners to put two individuals together for the purposes of rearing children. "If a owner had a big woman slave and she had a little man for her husban' and de owner had a big man slave, dey would make de little husban' leave, and make de woman let de big man be her husban', so ders be big chillen which dey could sell well."[19]

Sam Jones Washington

Additionally, former slave Silvia King recalled being subjected to a forced relationship and ex-slaves Josephine Howard, Sam Jones Washington, and Sarah Ford recalled stories told to them by their respective parents about how their former owners chose mates for them. King indicated that she was stolen from Africa, processed through New Orleans, and eventually became the property of a man she called "Marse Jones." She also said she had a husband and three children before being abducted, but she still found herself in a forced relationship. "After 'while, Marse Jones say to me, 'Silvia, am you married?' I tells him I got a man and chillens back in the old country, but he don't understand my talk and I has a man give to me. I don't bother with dat nigger's name much, he jes' Bob to me."[20]

Howard indicated that her parents were put together "like hosses or cattle." Washington also commented that his mother and father were placed into a forced union and said he did not even know who his real father was. "I don't know my pappy. Him am what dey calls de travelin' nigger. Dey have him come for service and when dey gits what dey wants, he go back to his massa. De women on Massa Young place not married."[21]

Ford said that her owner, Kit Patterson, controlled when and who they married. Ford's mother told her that Patterson did not care about slave relationships; he just wanted to add to his stock. "She say de white folks don't let de slaves what works in de field marry none, de jus' puts a man and breedin' woman together like mules. Iffen the woman don't like the man it don't make no diff'rence, she better go or dey gives her a hidin.'"[22]

The idea of the master forcing one slave to marry another without their mutual consent and slave breeding are perhaps two of the most contentious subjects in slave historiography. Robert William Fogel and John Boles vehemently argued that there was no such thing as slave breeding in any form. Fogel used economic models to disprove the existence of breeding, believing instead in the natural reproduction of blacks.[23] Boles agreed and stated that there is a lack of reliable evidence that breeding was nothing more than a tool of nineteenth-century abolitionists to decry slavery. He found that reliable evidence that slave owners, as a general practice, interfered with the sex lives of slaves so as to maximize reproduction did not exist. Furthermore, Boles argued that there is no evidence of a gross sexual imbalance that would found if slave stud farms existed. Rather than focusing on the possibility of breeding as a cause of black demographic changes, Boles challenged historians to examine other factors, such changing labor needs, to account for slave population increases.[24]

However, there are some historians who disagree with Boles and argue that the practice of breeding humans as one would breed animals to produce a desired offspring did exist, and the practice had the most detrimental effect on the slave population. Historian Paul Escott found that breeding was often used as a mechanism to control not only the slave population but also as a way of creating a new breed of slave. In *Slavery Remembered*, Escott found that slave owners routinely manipulated the sexual activities of their slaves, and particularly, their female slaves. Extremely fertile females, sometimes referred to as "breed women," were highly valued by the slave owner for their ability to successfully carry and deliver numerous healthy slave children. Such women often received light duty and an extended period for convalescence after a successful birth. Likewise, those male slaves used as breeders were known as a "stockman," "travelin' nigger," or "breedin' nigger." Escott argued that these men, like their female counterparts, received extra privileges that may have included money and or multiple wives.[25]

Likewise, historian Frank Tannenbaum even found that some slave states were considered "breeding states." In these states, breeding was a necessary system based purely on the economic resources generated. Furthermore, Tannenbaum found that breeding reduced the black female in stature to that of a breeding animal whose only value was in the number of healthy children she could produce.[26]

Further proof of the widespread belief in breeding as a detriment to the black community can be found in the words of alleged slave owner Willie Lynch, who suggested to his audience in 1712 to use several techniques that would maintain blacks in a permanent underclass position. He urged his audience to breed slaves but to keep the male slaves from developing any kind of paternal instinct. When this occurred, slave females were forced to depend on the slave owner for the protection of herself and her children.

Additionally, Lerone Bennett acknowledged that many slave "apologists" deny the existence of breeding, but he said they ignore the evidence from the slave owners themselves. He pointed to the numerous advertisements that listed black females for sale as "stock and breeding Negroes." Additionally, Bennett commented that most advertisements used terms that left little doubt as to the intended purpose of some black females. These included "She is a number one girl," "This is truly a number one woman," "Breeding slaves," "child-bearing women," and "breeding period."[27]

Although studies of black families indicated that the typical norms of the slave community involved monogamy, even if the partner was not of one's choosing, it had little influence on the ever-present threat of the sexual liberties taken by the slave owner.[28] A female slave was placed in the owner's house with the intended purpose of indoctrinating her as his mistress. The slave owner's wife was often aware of his dalliances, but she frequently found herself powerless to do anything about it. Furthermore, instead of blaming the husband, wives typically blamed the slave for being a promiscuous temptress.[29]

There were instances when the slave owner brazenly had intimate relationships with a female slave, regardless if she was married or not.[30] Such relationships between white males and slave females rested on the white male's assertion that slavery meant ownership, which implied they owned every aspect of the slave, even their sexuality. Furthermore, there is sufficient evidence to suggest that many white males purchased female slaves merely for the purposes of having sex. Female slaves understood that any rejection of the slave owner's sexual advances could mean the possibility of severe punishments that might include beatings and separations from family.[31]

Former slave Jack Maddox recalled how his owner, Judge Maddox, brought home a "purty mulatto gal, real bright and long black hair what was purty straight." The judge told his wife he bought this slave to help her do "needlework." The wife immediately noticed the attention this female slave received from her husband, and one day when the judge was away, the wife cut this slave's hair "to the skull." Jack believed the judge brought this female slave to the plantation for his own sexual reasons. "I do know white men got plenty chillen by the nigger women. They didn't ask 'em. They jes' took 'em."[32]

Rosa Maddox, Jack's wife and a former slave herself, confirmed her husband's statement that it was not uncommon for a white male to be sexually involved with a female slave. "White man laid a nigger gal when he wanted her. Some them white men had a plumb cravin' for the other color. But Master (Dr. Andrews) was a good man and I never heard of him botherin' any nigger woman. But they was some red-headed neighbors what had a whole crop of red-headed slaves."[33]

Former slave Mary Reynolds recalled how Dr. Kilpatrick, her former owner, once brought home a "yaller gal" from Baton Rouge and told his wife she was going to help with the sewing. "He builds her a house 'way from the quarters and she done fine sewin' for the whites." The implication being that Kilpatrick built this woman a house away from the quarters and she was more than just another black seamstress, and the other slaves knew it. "[T]his yaller gal breeds so fast and gits a mess of white young'uns."[34]

Many of the former slaves interviewed in Texas indicated that their fathers were white and as a result remembered enjoying privileges other slave children did not. For example, ex-slave Cato Carter indicated he received preferential treatment because his father was also his owner. As a house slave, Carter clearly enjoyed unchallenged access in and around the owner's house, where he also had his own room. In describing his treatment, Carter said, "They was allus good to me, 'cause I's one of their blood. They never hit me a lick or slapped me once, and told me they'd never sell me away from them."[35]

Even though Carter recalled the paternalism of his former owners, others recalled the helplessness felt by adult slaves as they were incapable of protecting their children. Furthermore, the plantation system prevented adult slaves from exercising any type of control over their own labor, let alone the labor of their children.[36] It was the master, not the parents, who determined where and when children would enter into the plantation's work system. Kenneth Stampp and Sylviane Diouf found most children entered the labor system by carrying water and food into the fields. By the time they reached ten or twelve years of age, those identified as field hands began working alongside adults, but they were not required to produce as much as adults. By the time they reached their eighteenth birthday, slave children were then classified as prime field hands and would continue as such until they reached old age.[37]

One of the most traumatic aspects of slavery involved the treatment of children fathered by the white masters. Frederick Douglass commented that slave women were unable to defend themselves from the lusts of the slave owners, and children so produced served two purposes. The first was the obvious satisfying of his lusts. The second was the continued production of slaves as chattel because the children of such unions still followed the servile nature that bound their mothers.

However, some ex-slaves indicated that some slave owners had little conscience when it came to punishing or selling their slave children. Agatha Babino recalled that "Some masters have chillen by slaves. Some sold dere own chillen."[38] As the daughter of her master, Annie Osborne remembered her mother working in the field, while she took care of the master's children in the big house. Even though she did not come to Texas from Atlanta until after emancipation, she nonetheless remembered how she was treated during slavery. "My white folks didn't teach us nothin', 'cept how they could put the whip on us. . . . We was treated jus' like animals, but some owners treated they

Anne Clark

stock better 'n' old Tom Bias (her master/father) handled my folks." She said Bias would often hit her with a leather strap and once beat her so severely that she could not see out of her right eye for two months.[39]

Not only was the work of the slave often grueling, lasting anywhere from ten to fourteen hours a day, but Sarah Ford also told her WPA interviewer that her master controlled when and who they married. Her master was Kit Patterson and he owned a plantation near West Columbia, located south of Houston. Ford's mother told her that Patterson did not care about the relationships of slaves; he just wanted to add to his stock.

Frederick Douglass also commented that some slave owners sold their slave children as soon as possible, whereas others punished them as they would any other slave.[40] Former slave mother Anne Clark sadly remembered her mother telling her that their owner, Captain Clark, sold her half-siblings. "My mama had two white chillen by marster and they were sold as slaves."[41]

Such separations were one of the unfortunate realities of slavery and often used as a form of punishment.[42] Still, historian Sally McMillen argued that familial separations often led to an unusual independence among slave females. As a result, they formed intense attachments to their children and prepared themselves for the inevitable day when they would be left to raise their children alone.[43]

For female slaves, being separated from husbands and children occurred too frequently. In *Slavery in America*, historian Robert Liston found that nearly 20 percent of slave marriages were destroyed through the sale of a spouse. Also the selling of children from parents became commonplace, as much for the economic benefit as for the measure of control it allowed the master to exert over his slaves.[44] Historian Timothy Dwight Weld found that even when the slave family did belong to the same owner, it did not prevent them from being sold as a unit, or individually, in a manner similar to livestock.[45]

Ex-slaves Carter Jackson, Sarah Asley, and Stearlin Arnwine each recollected for their respective interviewers their experiences of either being sold or witnessing others being sold away from the family. Jackson told his interviewer his anguish at watching his mother sold away from her children. "Me and four of her chillen standin' by when mammy's sold for $500. Cryin' didn't stop 'em from sellin' our mammy 'way from us."[46] Arnwine also remembered the auction block and said, "I seed slaves for sale on de auction block. They sol' 'em 'cordin' to strengt' and muscles. They was stripped to de wais'. I seed the women and little chillum cryin' and beggin' not to be separated, but it didn' do no good. They had to go."[47] Lastly, Ashley recalled her feelings at being sold on the auction block in New Orleans. "Us family was sep'rated. My two sisters and my papa was sold to a man in Georgia. Den dey put me on a block and bid me off. Dat in New Orleans and I scairt and cry, but dey put me up dere anyway."

However, former slave Josephine Howard said that her mother's owner decided to relocate from Alabama to Texas, which meant the permanent separation of her parents because her father belonged to a different owner. "One mornin' we is all herded up and mammy cryin' and say dey gwine to Texas, but can't take pappa. He don't 'long to dem. Dat de lastes' time we ever seen papa. Us and de women am put in wagons but de men slaves am chained together and has to walk."[48]

Likewise, Thomas Johns recalled that his mother and older half-sister were separated from her first husband when they were sold from Virginia to Alabama. Hagar Lewis was separated from her family when she was given to her owner's daughter as a wedding present.[49] John Barker and Toby Jones both remembered observing slaves being sold like animals. Barker said, "I seed slaves sold and they was yoked like steers and sold by pairs sometimes."[50] Jones recalled, "I seed slaves sold, and they'd make them clean up good and grease their hands and face so they'd look real fat, and sell them off. Of course, most the niggers didn't know their parents or what chillen was theirs. The white folks didn't want them to git 'tached to each other."[51]

Former slave Lucinda Elder told her interviewer that her father lived on an adjacent plantation from her and her mother, but he "come to see mama on

Wednesday and Sat'day nights."[52] It was also not uncommon for married slaves to live on separate plantations, although many owners preferred their slaves to marry on the same plantation.[53] Even when married slaves were on the same plantation, slave fathers or husbands had little parental influence in the family unit. Slavery virtually destroyed the traditional roles of paternal responsibility of the black male because he was unable to support or protect his family. That responsibility was assumed by the slave owner.[54]

Nonetheless, the narratives of ex-slaves Arnwine, Louise Mathews, Annie Row, and Maggie Jackson illustrated how common it was for slave fathers not to live on the same plantation with his wife and children. Arnwine, born near Jacksonville, Texas, said he knew of his father, but he did not live on the same plantation with him, his mother, and other siblings. "I don' know whar my pappy come from."[55] Mathews told her interviewer, "My pappy and mammy don't live together, 'cause pappy am own by Massa Jack Hooper. Massa Turner done marry dem. Mostest de cullud folks jus' lives together by 'greement den, but massa have de cer'mony."[56]

Born near Rusk, Texas, Row, told her interviewer that her father came to visit them with or without permission from his owner. "Marster Charley owned my mammy and my sisters and two brothers but pappy was owned by Marster John Kluck, and his place was 'bout five mile from Marster Charley's plantation. My pappy was 'lowed a pass every two weeks for to come and see him's family, but him seen us more often that that, 'cause he sneak off every time him have de chance."[57] Finally, Jackson, born in Cass County, Texas, told his interviewer, "My mama was Sam Oliver's slave, but my pappa lived a mile away with Masta Sam Carlow."[58]

There is no question that slave children were often considered assets by their owners.[59] Evidence also suggests that some owners purposefully had sex with their female slaves with the intent on producing children. Interviewed in Fort Worth, ex-slave Fred Brown told a story of how the overseer on the Brown plantation often controlled whom the slaves married. "He am used for to father de chillum. Him picks de portly and de healthy women dat am to rear de porty chillun. . . . Dem dat him pick he overlooks, and not 'low dem to marry or to go round with other nigger men. If dey do, its whippin' sho'. De massa raises some fine, portly chillen, and dey sel' some, after dey's half grown, for $500 and sometimes more."[60]

However, not all familial separations were caused by whites. Ex-slave Zek Brown was born in Tennessee and separated from his family when he was ten years old because he wanted to teach his mother a lesson. However, he ended up hiding in a covered wagon destined for Texas and never saw his parents again.

> De way I leaves home am dis. One day mammy teachin' school and me and my sister am home, and I 'cides she need de haircut. She want it, too, So I gits de shears and goes to work and after I works a while de job don't look so good, so I cuts some more and de it look worse and I tries to fix it and first thing I knows dere ain't no hair left to cut. When mammy come home she pays me for de work with de rawhide whip and dat hurts my feelin's so bad I 'cides ti git even by runnin' 'way a few days.[61]

There is little question that whites controlled every aspect of the slaves' existence through coercion and violence, but many slaves still found ways to create and maintain familial relationships.[62] Unfortunately, the many of the former slaves in Texas remembered their family's lives as anything but stable. Lulu Wilson from Dallas said, "Ain't got no brudders or sisters that I knows 'bout. All a slave have to go by am what de white folks tell him 'bout his kinfolks."[63] This sentiment is found throughout the Texas slaves' narratives. The ex-slaves often told of their relationships with parents, especially their mothers, and grandparents. However, many also indicated they either did not know or had little knowledge of their fathers.

Born in Ohio, and interviewed in Houston, Texas, ex-slave John Barker described himself as a, "Malagasser [Madagascar] nigger." He also recalled knowing his grandparents and how his grandfather attempted to runaway from the plantation, but their owner tracked him and found him one hundred miles away and brought him back.[64] Ex-slave Gus Bradshaw also remembered not knowing his father, but he had a profound relationship with his grandmother whom he said always told him to be respectful of others. "My grandma (Maria Gloster) say to me, 'Gus, don't run your mouth too much and allus have manners to whites and blacks.'"[65]

Former slaves Priscilla Gibson, William Byrd, James Hayes, and Ellen Butler told their interviewers they had no real knowledge of their fathers. Gibson, born in Mississippi, but brought to Texas by slave owner Jesse Puckett, commented to her interviewer that her father was an Indian or a white man. "Mammy's

John Barker

name was Mary Puckett, but I never seed my father as I knows of, Don' know if he was a whole Injun or part white man."⁶⁶ Byrd was born near Madisonville, Texas, said that he believed his owner, Sam Byrd was his father, but he could not confirm this. "My mother's name was Fannie and I dunno pappy's name, 'cause my mother allus say she found me a stray in the woods. I allus 'lieves my master was my pappy, but I never did know for sho.'"⁶⁷ Lastly, both Hayes and Butler simply commented that they did not know their fathers.⁶⁸

Conversely, some of Texas's former slaves knew the identity of their fathers, but for one reason or another had no relationship with them. Born in Wharton County, ex-slave Ben Kinchlow recalled his mother, Lizaer Moore was half-white and his father was a "white man of that same county. I don't know anything about my father. He was a white man, I know that."⁶⁹ Ex-slave Rosanna Frazier was born in Mississippi and said, "My daddy name Jerry Durden and after I's born they brings us all to Texas, but my daddy belong to de Neylands, so we loses him."⁷⁰

Former slave Aunt Pinkie Kelly, born in Brazoria County, said, "My mammy's name was Harriet Jackson and she was born on de same plantation. My pappy's name was Dan, but folks called him Good Cheer. He druv oxen and one day they show me him and say he my pappy, and so I guess he was, but I can't tell much about him, 'cause chillen then didn't know their pappys like chillen do now."

Ex-slave Phoebe Henderson was born in Georgia but brought to Panola County, Texas, in 1859, "I was bo'n a slave of the Bradley family in Macon, Georgia. My father's name was Anthony Hubbard and he belonged to the Hubbards in Georgia. He was a young man when I lef' Georgia and I never heard from him since. I 'members my mother; she had a gang of boys. Marster Hill brought her to Texas with us."[71]

As an institution, slavery was designed to maximize the labor of slaves to receive the most profits. The idea of slaves living within the concept of a family was rarely important to the slave owner. Nonetheless, slaves throughout the South and Texas were able to replicate the family unit despite the forced sexual relationships, separations, and the ability of the slave owner to obliterate that unit at a whim.

SEVEN

THE CONDITIONS OF SLAVERY

Stable black families were often anomalies during slavery. However, the wretched conditions under which blacks lived were fairly consistent. Historians have documented the diets, clothing, housing, and the limited leisure of slaves (during which they grew their own food and practiced their own religion), thus illustrating the conditions of the black community. Many in Texas' black community did succeed in creating an atmosphere of family and community that extended to the ways they ate, the clothes they wore, the houses they lived in, and the ways they spent they precious few moments away from the watchful eyes of whites.

Many of the former slaves indicated in their oral narratives that nearly all of their food supplies were either grown or manufactured on their respective plantation. Some of the plantation slaves made shoes and leather goods from available cattle; slaves placed the wool from the sheep they grew on spinning looms and made their own clothes; and slaves raised or tended to chickens and turkeys for food. As such, some said that they were well fed as slaves and that food was never in short supply.[1]

The basic slave diet typically consisted of corn meal and salt pork or bacon. Financially, the average slave owner usually spent less than thirty dollars annually per slave. Although this may not seem like a huge financial commitment when compared to modern food prices, it was by antebellum standards. As a result, the nourishment of slaves was still a significant investment for most slave owners.[2]

Such investment supports the argument presented by historian Peter Kolchin that slaves enjoyed an abundance of food. Author Richard Steckel supports

Kolchin's argument in principle, but he found that only adult slaves had enough food whereas slave children were poorly fed.[3] Still other historians maintained that it was rare for slaves to have adequate or nutritious food.[4] Some of this discrepancy can be attributed to how slave owners distributed food to their slaves. Some masters provided their slaves a weekly food allowance, whereas others provided an allowance and also permitted the slaves to hunt, fish, and grow their own vegetables.[5]

Former slave Lucy Lewis indicated that the living conditions of the slaves on the McNeel Plantation were often better than what she was enjoying in the 1930s. "We used to git lots to eat, greens and suet, fish from de ribber, cornmeal and plenty of sugar, even in de war time."[6] Likewise former slaves Tom Holland, Charly Mitchell, and Lorenza Ezell concurred that their former masters fed them well during slavery. Holland's former master–owner allowed his slaves to eat wild meat, possum, rabbit, fish, and cornbread, whereas Mitchell said, his former owner, Nat Thurman, provided his slaves with plenty of food and felt that considering the fact that he was a slave, he remembered his quantity of food was better than many other slaves in the area. The fact that the distribution of food was, as was everything else during slavery, dependent entirely on the whims of the slave owner is supported by the narrative of Ezell. He recalled how his former owner, Ned Lipscomb, allowed his slaves to raise their own gardens that they were then allowed to sell in local markets. He also commented that most slave owners in their area did not allow slaves to grow their own gardens or provide them with sufficient food. As a result, Ezell recalled that many slaves were forced to steal food to survive.[7]

Because many of the former slaves interviewed in Texas were children when emancipated, they remembered what the food distribution process was like for slave children. The former slaves in Texas generally commented that slave children generally had enough food even though they usually ate separately from their parents and other adults. For example, Yach Stringfellow, born in Brenham, Texas, said the slave children on Frank Humbert's plantation ate in a trough. He said, "Us chillen had a long, seeped-out dish on a split leg table. What we had to eat was dumped in dat trough and use ate it lie slop.... But it sho' taste good when you been huntin' for eggs or calves or gittin' in chips or breakin' bresh."[8] Born on the Rimes Plantation, which was located near Newton, Texas, Abram Sells, like Stringfellow, said as a child he also ate out of a trough.

> They fed all us negger chillen in big trough make out'n wood. They put it under a tree in the shade in summer time and give each chile a wood spoon, then mix all the food up in the trough and us goes to eatin'. Mos' the food was potlicker, jes' common old potlicker; turnip green and the juice. Irish 'taters and the juice, cabbages and peas and beans, jes' anything what make potlicker.[9]

Former slave Laura Smalley also recalled all the slave children coming together in a house or the "slop room place" and eating out of a structure she described as, "a hog pit, a hog trough."[10]

Although many former slaves remembered that they enjoyed a variety of foods, studies of the slaves' diet often indicate the foods they ate had marginal nutritional value. In his study of slavery, historian Robert Liston found that the diets of a majority of slaves were never balanced or nutritious. This led to frequent illnesses and other health-related problems. "[E]ven when the food provided enough bulk to fill [the slave's] stomach, he [or she] never had a balanced diet. Vitamin deficiencies and disease resulted."[11] Although some former slaves throughout the country recalled having sufficient food to eat, most said they were barely fed. Even with their weekly rations and the ability to grow their own food, many slaves recalled that they still did not have enough food to eat.[12] As former Texas slave Ezell described, this lack of food caused many slaves to steal food from their owners whenever they could.[13]

Certainly many of Texas' former slaves said they had enough food, but others, in addition to Ezell, definitely recalled either being constantly hungry or were aware of slaves who were often hungry, which led them to sometimes steal food. For example, former slave Betty Powers said that the weekly rations they received were often not enough.

> All de rations measure out Sunday mornin' and it have to do for de week. It am not 'nough for heavy eaters and we has to be real careful or we goes hungry. We has meat and cornmeal and 'lasses and 'taters and peas and beans and milk. Dem short rations causes plenty trouble, 'cause de niggers has to steal food and it am de whippin' if dey gits

cotched. Dey am in a fix if dey can't work for bein' hungry, 'cause it am de whippin' den, sho' so dey has to steal, and most of 'em did and takes de whippin'. Dey has de full stomach anyway.[14]

Born in Alabama, Jenny Proctor said her former master relocated to Leon County, Texas, and she recalled the slaves were often hungry. She remembered stealing food whenever the opportunity presented itself, regardless of the consequences. She recalled when she found a biscuit in the owner's home and ate it. To her dismay, the slave owner's wife returned a short time later and inquired to the whereabouts of the biscuit she left behind. Proctor said she admitted to eating the biscuit because she was hungry. Undaunted by her honesty, she recalled how the wife grabbed a nearby broom and began hitting her over the head while calling her a lowdown nigger.[15] Like Proctor, other former slaves admitted to stealing food. Ex-slave Mary Reynolds said the slaves on the Kilpatrick plantation often had insufficient food rations and were also frequently hungry. She said whenever she could steal "a 'tater," she would by first hiding it and then returning to eat it when she could.[16]

Like their diets, most studies of slave clothing usually found it to be inadequate.[17] Slave females were typically responsible for making the clothes, and in some cases, the shoes for her family. On those plantations where the owner provided clothing, slaves received one set of winter and summer clothing. Male slaves usually received two suits (shirt and pants) per year and a single pair of shoes. Women, especially those working in or near the main house, might receive castoffs from their mistress.[18] Children, regardless of gender, usually wore a shirt with no pants or shoes until they were generally about ten to twelve years of age.[19]

Historian Kenneth Stampp argued that the lack of clothing had little to do with the cruelty of the slave owner and more to do with economics because they did not want to spend excess money for clothes. Although Stampp did find that some slaves were fortunate to have what they considered "fine" clothes, it was the exception.[20]

The narratives from ex-slaves Francis Hawley, Abram Sells, Stearlin Arnwine, Tom Holland, and Lucy Lewis illustrate that the variety of clothing worn by Texas' former slaves was less than "fine." Hawley said that the clothing of most male slaves was unserviceable and that children usually went about the plantation practically naked until the age of twelve.[21] Sells indicated that "boys and girls all dress jes' alike, one long shirt or dress. They call it a shirt iffen a boy wear it and call it a dress iffen the gal war it."[22] Arnwine remembered, "I wore my first pants when I was fourteen years ole, and they stung 'till I was mis'ble. The cloth was store bought but mammy made the pants at home. Mammy made my first shoes, we called 'em red rippers."[23] Holland, born in Walker County, Texas, said he wore shirts but did not have shoes until after freedom.[24] Conversely, Lewis recalled her former owner, Johnny McNeel, provided the slaves on the McNeel plantation near Pleasant Grove, Texas, with clothes and shoes. Furthermore, she also remembered McNeel giving his slaves money with which they bought clothes. "We used to wear good clothes—real purty clothes . . . and sho' 'nough, I had some purty red russett shoes."[25]

Although slaves often commented that food and clothing were inadequate, there was no consensus on the opinions of slave housing. Some considered the homes they lived in to be satisfactory, whereas others said their housing resembled "stalls like pens they use for cattle."[26] Most slaves lived in cabins or large multifamily barracks that were typically twenty feet square single room structures with a single window and sometimes a fireplace for heating and cooking.[27] Additionally, the cabins were most often built out of material that provided basic shelter from the elements but hardly sturdy enough to last several seasons. Most often the floors were dirt, and wooden floors were considered a luxury.[28] Historian Lerone Bennett quoted a former slave who said "Everything happened in that one room—birth, sickness, death—everything."[29]

Texas' former slaves generally indicated that they considered their quarters adequate, and most were made of logs or pine boards tied together with mortar and generally described as "comfortable."[30] Both former slaves Mary Ann Patterson and Cinto Lewis even recalled that their former slave quarters were comparable to the homes most blacks found themselves in during the 1930s.[31]

Not only were the slaves' quarters often comfortable, but some of Texas' former slaves also remembered that they slept on mattresses. For example, Rosa Maddox said her former owner, Dr. Andrews, treated his slaves well and provided more than adequate housing. "Dr. Andrews was good to us and give us good li'l cabins and cotton mattresses and blankets."[32] Likewise, former slave Ellen Payne also remembered sleeping on "good wood beds and hay mattresses."[33]

However, not all slave housing was adequate. Ex-slave James W. Smith from Fort Worth described the slave quarters as, "built cheap, though, no money, only time for buildin' am de cost."[34] Ex-slave John Sneed said that children slept on the floor and the adults slept on some type of crude and uncomfortable bed.[35] In discussing the types of furniture in the slave quarters, ex-slave Abram Sells said

> The beds had jes' one leg. They bored two hole in the wall up in the corner and stuck two pole in them holes and lay plank on that like slats and pile lots of pine straw on that like slats and pile lots of pine straw on that. . . . They spread a homemake blanket or quilt on that and sometime four or five li'l niggers slep' in there to keep us warm.[36]

Whether or not the slaves' housing was adequate was inconsequential to the owner. The time spent in the quarters was limited because slaves were expected to work or perform other required duties. Texas' former slaves also indicated their masters expected field slaves to begin their work day before sunrise, and often the work day would not end until night fall. As a result, they said there was little time for leisure activities. Former slave Green Cumby, born near Henderson, Texas, said, "We didn't have no gardens ourselves, 'cause we wouldn't have time to work in dem. We worked all day in de fields and den was so tired we couldn't do nothin' more."[37] Former slave Aunt Pinkie Kelly's recollections of slavery were similar to those of Cumby. "Most I 'members 'bout them times is work. 'cause we's put out in de fields befo' day and come back after night. Then we has to shell a bushel of corn befo' we goes to bed and we was so tired we didn't have time for nothin.'"[38] Lastly, ex-slave John Barker stated, "I 'spect dere was 'bout 40 or 50 acres in de plantation. Dey worked and worked and didn't have no dances or church. Dances nothing!"[39]

However, there were instances where they recalled enjoying various leisure activities that included dances, hunting, fishing, gardening, and church services. The former slaves used these activities to bond with one another and mostly occurred on their plantation. Furthermore, there were instances when slave owners allowed their slaves to interact with those on other plantations thus uniting slaves on different plantations into a wider slave community with a given region.

When asked to recall any leisure activities during slavery, Mrs. John Barclay replied, "We had to work if there was work to be done. When we got

Anderson and Minerva Edwards

caught up den we could have time off." Most of Texas' former slaves responded to the question about leisure activities in much the same manner as Barclay. Historians find that the most recognized activity was the Saturday night dances. Some slave owners approved of the dances and provided slaves with passes to go to other plantations where the dances were held. However, others vehemently opposed such gatherings as a means of keeping slaves isolated from each other and focused solely on their work.[40]

Still, many of the former slaves made the instruments they played and often recalled that they danced well into the Saturday nights. Anderson and Minerva Edwards told their interviewer, "On Saturday nights we'd sing and dance and we made our own instruments, which was gourd fiddles and quill flutes."[41] Fred

James Jackson

Albert Hill

Brown said his former owner, John Brown, also allowed his slaves to have parties on the plantation. "We is 'lowed to have parties and de dance and we has for music, sich as de banjo and de jew's harp and a 'cordian. Dey dance de promenade and de jog."[42] James Jackson commented that he was too young to remember specifics about the Saturday dances, but he knew the adult slaves enjoyed themselves. "Dey had meetin' and dances Saturday nights. I was too young to 'member jus' what de songs was, but dey had a fiddle and played all night long."[43] Lastly, Wes Brady recalled how his former owner, John Jeems, not only allowed his slaves to enjoy parties on Saturdays, but also often joined in the revelry. "We had parties Saturday nights and massa come out and showed us new steps."[44]

However, not all Texas' slave owners allowed such activities own the plantation. For example, former slave Charlotte Beverly remembered that her master would not allow the slaves to dance on his plantation, but he would give them passes to go to the plantation where her father lived where they were allowed to dance.[45] Likewise, ex-slave Albert Hill's master was another who discouraged dances and parties, but, like Beverly's owner, would provide his slaves passes to dance elsewhere. Hill said, "We dances near all night Saturday night, but we ha to stay way in the back where de white folks can't hear us. Sometimes we has de fiddle and de banjo and does we cut dat chicken wing and shuffle! We sho' does."[46]

Former slave Campbell Davis told his interviewer that his slave owner gave them Friday afternoons and Saturdays off. On Fridays, the women washed clothes while the men either fished or hunted. But on Saturday nights they danced. "Sometimes dey have parties Saturday night and couples git on de floor and have music of de fiddle and banjo." He could also recall one song

Hop light, li'l lady,
The cake all dough,
Don't mind de whether,
Jus' so de wind don't blow.⁴⁷

Like Campbell, many former slaves said that they only worked half-days on Fridays and were free all day Saturday. In addition to parties, many former slaves said these were the only days their former owners gave them to cultivate their own crops. There were examples from the former slaves where they not only had gardens, but they and their slave owners also profited from them.

Ex-slave Will Adams told his interviewer how his former owner, Dave Cavin, only allowed them to cultivate their own crops on Saturday. He said, "The hands worked from sun to sun. Massa give them li'l crops and let them work them on Saturday."⁴⁸ He continued by recalling that Cavin would sometimes buy the crops from his slaves. This provided the slaves with their own money that was often used to purchase clothes. "Lots saved money and bought freedom 'fore the war was over."⁴⁹

Charlotte Beverly

Former slave Charlotte Beverly remembered that her former owner, Captain Pankey, also allowed his slaves to grow their own crops, which provided them their own income on his plantation in Montgomery County, Texas. However, the only time they had to work their own crops was in the middle of the night. "Old marster used to let he slaves have extry cotton patch to themselves and they worked it by the moonlight. They could sell that cotton and have the money for themselves."⁵⁰

Ex-slave Pauline Johnson also recollected how her father worked his own garden on Sundays, and his crops gave him enough money to buy shoes and clothes. "Us daddy he work de ground he own on Sunday and sold the things to buy us shoes to put on us feet and clothes. The white folks didn't give us clothes but they let him have all the money he made in his own plot to get them."⁵¹

Like Adams, Beverly, and Johnson, ex-slave Ellen Payne recalled how her parents also worked in the fields during the day, "from sun to sun," but worked at night to make their own money. She said they cultivated their own piece of land, hunted, fished, made baskets, chairs, and knitted socks for sale. "My daddy allus had some money, 'cause he made baskets and chair bottoms and sold them, and Master Evans give every slave a patch to work and they could sell it and keep the money."[52]

Although many slaves were allowed to cultivate their own crops for sale as a way of making money, they still understood that they were still slaves and such privileges could be taken from them without notice.[53] Still, some historians found that when slave owners combined the task system with the opportunity to have their own land and money, it increased the slave's identification to the plantation. Historian Larry Hudson further argued that this benefited the slave owner in two ways. First, some slave owners would sell the crops harvested by the slaves and keep a percentage of the profits, which contributed to the overall profitability of the plantation. Secondly, slave owners believed the slaves were less likely to run when they felt a degree of autonomy on the plantation.[54]

Even though times for leisure activities were infrequent, slaves successfully used the time to develop a sense of community that allowed them to survive the hardships of slavery. In addition to allowing parties and the cultivation of small gardens, whites rarely denied their slaves the opportunity to practice some form of religion; in fact, they often encouraged slaves to convert to Christianity as a necessary conversion process from savagery to civilization. Even on those plantations where it was not openly allowed, slaves still exercised some religious practices.[55] Historians Eugene Genovese and Joan Martin also found that slave owners often used religion as a form of social control. Slaves were taught to obey their masters as the only way to receive a reward in heaven, even if it was not the white man's heaven.[56] The most common religious message preached to black slaves was that of salvation for unbridled obedience. Historian William Freehling stated, "The minister's most powerful message was that of salvation, with both blacks and whites, involved renouncing such alleged sins (for example, stealing, lying, sabotage, and disobedience), trading behavior that supposedly ought to shame any Christian for an ecstatic embrace of Christ."[57]

Historian Peter Kolchin found that slave owners often encouraged their slaves' spirituality.⁵⁸ In Texas, former slave William Mathews said Buck Adams, his owner, could, "out-mean the debbil heself." Likewise, Mathews described Adams' wife as, "most hard as he was." Mathews said that his former masters cared little about their spirituality and that the slaves were made to escort the Adamses to church but were not allowed to enter the building.

Daniel Phillips

> Sometimes, dey make de slaves go to church. De white folks sot up fine in dere carriage and drive up to de door and git de slaves out of one cabin, den git the slaves out of de nex' cabin, and keep it up till dey gits dem all. Den all de slaves walks front de carriage till dey gits to church. De slaves sot outside under de shade trees. If de preacher talk real loud, you can hear him out de window.⁵⁹

Nevertheless, many of Texas' former slaves recollected being encouraged to attend church services by their masters. They also said these services were segregated because the slaves were forced to sit in a separate area of the church. Former slave Daniel Phillips told how his owner, Dr. Thomas Daily, encouraged his slaves to go to church as a means of behavior control. "We walks fo' miles to de church. De white folks sits in the front and de cullud folks sits back by de do.'"⁶⁰

Ex-slave Carey Davenport related that her former owner, John Mann, allowed various preachers to come to his plantation in Walker County, Texas, and let his slaves participate in the services. "I don't 'member no cullud preachers in slavery times. The white Methodist circuit riders come round on horseback and preach. There was a big box house for a church house and the cullud folks sit off in one corner of the church."⁶¹

Former slaves Martha Patton and Henry Lewis told their interviewers that the slaves on their respective plantations were also encouraged to attend church services, but theirs was segregated. Patton remembered whites having their church services on Sunday mornings and that the slaves were not permitted to hold church services until Sunday evening.[62]

Born in Jefferson County, Texas, Lewis said, "Old massa 'low us to praise Gawd but lots of massas didn't 'low dem to git on de kness. Us have churchhouse and de white folks go in de mornin' and us go in de mornin' and us go after dinner." He sang the following song:

> My knee bones achin',
> My body's a rackin' with pain,
> I calls myself de chile of Gawd,
> Heaven am my aim.
> If you don't 'lieve I's a chile of Gawd,
> Jis' meet me on dat other shore,
> Heaven is my home.
> I calls myself a chile of Gawd,
> I's a long time on my way,
> But Heaven am my home.[63]

Whether the church services were segregated or not, the religious message the former slaves most often recalled involved obeying their former masters. Ex-slave Richard Carruthers, born in Tennessee, but brought to Bastrop County, Texas, by Billy Coats said, "When the white preacher come he preach and pick up his Bible and claim he gittin the text right out from the good book and he preach: 'The Lord say, don't you niggers steal chickens from your missus. Don't you steal YOUR MARSTER'S hawgs.' That would be all he preach"[64]

Former slave Wayman Williams recalled even the black preachers exhorted the slaves to obey their masters and used the promise of salvation to control behavior on behalf of his former owners, Calvin and Julia Williams. Williams recalled a familiar religious theme

> Now, you no count niggers, what you mean stealin' de white folks chickens and watermillions? Dey ain't safe no longer dan de white man back am turned. Do you think Gawd would save you? No sir! You be turned into de pillar of salt iffen you don't stop you unrighteous ways and den where you be? You won't be dancin' or hear no chicken hollerin'. Come on into de pearly gates and live right. Leave

your stealin' and cussin' and dancin' to the debbil, and come to the mourners' bench.[65]

Although many slave owners encouraged religion on the plantation, the Texas slaves' narratives also provided numerous instances in which the former slaves recollected having to kept their religious services secret. Ex-slave Ellen Butler said of Richard Butler, her owner, "Massa never 'lowed us slaves go to church but they have big holes in the fields they gits down in and prays. They done that way 'cause the white folks didn't want them to pray. They used to pray for freedom."[66]

Born in Tennessee, Carruthers recalled how the slaves on Billy Coat's plantation used to sneak out and pray at night.

> Us niggers used to have a prayin' ground down in the hollow and sometime we come out of the field, between 11 and 12 at night, scorchin' and burnin' up with nothin' to eat, and we wants to ask the good Lawd to have mercy.... Some gits so joyous they starts to holler loud and we has to stop up they mouth. I see niggers git so full of the Lawd and so happy they draps unconscious.[67]

Former slaves Anderson and Minerva Edwards likewise commented, "When we prayed by ourse'ves we daren't let the white folks know it and we turned a wash pot down to the ground to cotch the voice. We prayed a lot to be free and the lord done heard us. We din't have no song books and the Lord done give us our songs and when we sing them at night it jus' whispering to nobody hear us." They sang the following spiritual for their interviewer:

> My knee bones am aching,
> My body's rackin with pain,
> I 'lieve I'm a chile of God,
> And this ain't my home,
> 'cause Heaven's my aim.[68]

Born near Jacksonville, Texas, ex-slave Stearlin Arnwine remembered praying and shouting at night. "The only chu'ch I knowed 'bout was when we'd git together in de night and have prayer meetin' and singin'. We use to go way out in de woods so de white folks wouldn't hear nothin'. Sometimes we'd stay nearly all night on Saturday, 'cause we didn' have to work Sunday."[69]

Sometimes praying out in the wood was not safe if the slave owner objected. That was why ex-slave John Price said the slaves on the Bryan plantation often posted a sentry to warn the others if whites approached.[70] Former slave Mary Reynolds said they used to sneak off the Kilpatrick plantation and prayed for food and "the end of Tribulation and the end of beatin's and for shoes that fit our feet."[71] Former slave Willie Ann Smith said, "sometimes we hums 'ligious songs low like when we's workin'. It was our way prayin' to be free, but the white folks didn't know it."[72]

Former slaves also indicated that whites observed some holidays on the plantation with food, dancing, and time off from work. Ex-slave Campbell Davis said Henry Hood, his owner, celebrated the Fourth of July and the entire plantation, black and white, would eat dinner together under the trees and "have cakes and pies and fancy cookin.'"[73] Davis also recollected the festivities that occurred during Christmas. "And on Christmas he [Hood] give us clothes and shoes and nuts and things and 'nother big dinner, and Christmas night de darkies sing songs for de white folks."[74]

Like Davis, William Byrd said Sam Byrd, his former owner, also made a big celebration of Christmas on his plantation near Madisonville, Texas. "On Christmas Marse Sam had a great big eggnog and kilt a big beef and had fireworks, and the nigger, he know Christmas was come, we had plenty to eat and eggnog and did 'bout what we pleased that day and New Year's. The white folks allus said what we'd do on them days we'd do all year. That's all follishment, but some still believes in it."[75]

Slaves were expected to be productive workers or incur severe repercussions. Everything surrounding the conditions of slavery was designed to reinforce the power of the master and the helplessness of the slave. Slave housing was seldom adequate, and unfortunately many former slaves commented that it was still better than their current living conditions in the 1930s. Adult slaves received "adequate" rations to prevent conditions of starvation, but the concept of nutrition was unheard of as the slaves' diet was woefully lacking. Another reinforcement of the owners' dominant position was the feeding of black children in a manner resembling that of hogs or some other four-legged creature.

Nonetheless, Texas' slaves recalled using their limited leisure time to either socialize or practice their own unique religious activities. Even though it was reported that whites generally encouraged religion as a form of social control, slaves still managed to incorporate aspects of worship that were uniquely theirs. This allowed the slave community to identify itself as something different when compared to the white community that oppressed them.

Therefore my heart exults, and with my song I shall thank Him.
Psalms 28:7

PART THREE

Freedom and the War of the Lost Cause

What do you remember about the war that brought your freedom? What did the slaves get after freedom?

"You should seed dem cullud folks. Dey jus' plumb shock. Dere faces long as dere arm, and so pester dey don't know what to say or do. Masas never say 'nother word and walks away. De cullud folks say 'Where we'uns gwine live? What we'uns gwine do?'"
    Elsie Reece

When the war finally was over, our old boss called us all up and had us to stand in abreast, and he stood on the gallery and he read the verdict to 'em, and said, 'Now, you can jes' work on if you want to, and I'll treat you jes' like I always did.' I guess when he said that they knew what he meant. The' wasn't but one family left with 'im. They stayed about two years. But the rest was just like birds, they jes' flew."
    Austin Grant

EIGHT

THE WAR AND EMANCIPATION

As war was becoming more and more inevitable, Abraham Lincoln adamantly stated his position that the federal government did not have the authority to eliminate slavery, but he was opposed to its expansion west of Texas. In his examination of Lincoln's war objectives, historian Ira Berlin quoted Lincoln: "It would be a war to restore national unity, a war in which slaves would be, at best, interested spectators whose status and circumstances would remain unchanged."[1] Still, Southern secessionists believed Lincoln's administration would not protect their rights as slave owners and they clung to the belief that slaves were property and the right to own slaves was protected by the by the Fifth Amendment of US Constitution. Furthermore, Southern leaders argued that the phrase, "All men are created equal," excluded blacks, and that the US government was founded by whites for the benefit of whites.[2]

Secessionists quickly gathered in Montgomery, Alabama, and created the Confederate States of America, seeing themselves in the same vein as the thirteen colonies during the American Revolution. However, unlike their predecessors, who took fourteen months to declare independence from Great Britain after the initial battles near Lexington and Concord, the Confederate States appeared within three months of Lincoln's 1860 election.[3]

As Southern states began filing out of the Union, Texas joined the secessionist movement. Texas experienced few military conflicts, but the war's impacts were still significant. Texas was on the western frontier of the Confederacy and vulnerable to attack from the north, west, and south. Indian raids became commonplace because state leaders were never successful in protecting frontier settlements. However, Texans had better luck defending the coastline after defeating the Union army in Galveston.[4]

Once the bombardment of Fort Sumter began, both Lincoln and Jefferson Davis were forced to recognize that neither had a sufficient army to fight a modern war. Nonetheless, Davis' Confederacy boasted of having some of the best young men ready to fight and defend their cause. Even with the apparent readiness of Southern white males to volunteer for military service, the Confederate government passed a conscription act for all males between eighteen and thirty-five years of age enlisting them in the army for the duration of the war.[5]

Fortunately, Lincoln was unable to keep blacks as merely "interested spectators." Thus, the ensuing war became synonymous with freedom because blacks throughout the country, free and slave, came to see it as the ability to live free of physical and emotional restraints and being paid a reasonable wage for their labor.[6] There were nearly 200,000 slaves in Texas, and even though the presence of Union armies in the state had little effect on slavery, most everyone, master and slave, knew some form of social, economic, and political change was on the horizon.[7]

Texas' former slaves recalled how their masters responded in much the same manner as others throughout the South. Some trained local volunteers for service in the state's militias; others collected food and supplies; and some actively participated in combat.[8] However, there were some white males in Texas that tried to avoid active military service altogether. For example, former slave Susan Ross said, "Lots of 'em didn't want to go, but dey has to."[9] Ellen Payne of Marshall, Texas, also commented that she was aware of many young white males who tried to get out of military service. "I 'member the white southern men folks run off to the bottoms to git 'way from war."[10] Lastly, Harrison Beckett told a second hand story of a slave owner's son who deserted his Confederate unit in Arkansas "when dat first cannon busts at Li'l Rock, he starts runnin' and never stops till he gits back home, I don't see how he could do det, 'cause Li'l Rock am way far off, but dat what dey say. Den de men comes to git 'serters and dey gits Li'l Ide and takes him back."[11]

In addition to how white Texans responded to the Civil War, most of the former slaves interviewed either remembered the war firsthand or were told how local slaves reacted to the conflict. For example, former slave Willie Forward commented that many slaves witnessed fighting as cooks, bodyguards, or nurses to their masters and other Confederate soldiers because he believed every slave owner took a slave to war with him.[12] Martin Jackson commented that he was not only aware of the implications of the Civil War, but he also recalled wanting the Confederacy to lose. Jackson said he followed his "young master" to war and eventually ended up with the First Texas Calvary. Furthermore, he remembered feeling that the North would win, but curiously said he did not want the First Texas Calvary defeated in the process. "I knew the Yanks were going to win, from the beginning. I wanted them to win

Martin Jackson

and lick us Southerners, but I hoped they was going to do it without wiping out our company." Jackson also commented that his father cautioned him that regardless of the outcome of the war, they were going to have to get along with whites after the war.[13]

Like Jackson, former slave William Adams also recalled how many of the more than one hundred slaves on the Davis plantation were taken and forced into service for the Confederates. Adams also remembered a white preacher telling the slaves that they should pray for the Confederacy to win or else they would be homeless, hungry, and live like "de wil' animals." Adams continued, saying this preacher asked the slaves to raise their hands if they supported the Confederacy, and said, "We all raised our hands 'cause we was skeered not to, but we sho' didn' wan' de South to win."[14]

Slaves not only experienced changes when forced into service for the Southern armies, but there were also many changes that occurred back on the farms and plantations. For example, Andy Anderson said that his slave owner began making preparations to join the Confederate army by hiring an overseer to manage the plantation in his absence. Anderson said life on the plantation changed after the overseer arrived: Their food rations were reduced but the new overseer demanded more production. He also said, "de hell start to pop . . . He half starve us niggers and he want mo' work and he start de whippin's."[15]

Conversely, former slaves Jack Bess, Abram Sells, and Henry Lewis said many slaves were aware of the war and the implication that it could result in their freedom. Bess said he heard about the war when the Confederate conscription began. Still, he said the war did not really mean anything to the slaves on the Bess ranch. "We didn' know hardly what dey was a talkin' 'bout 'cause we knowed dat would be too good to be true."[16]

Sells remembered other slaves talked quietly about what they were going to do when the war was over. They were nonetheless frightened by the possibility of freedom because they were unsure about what they would do or go. Still, in retrospect, Sells commented, "No, I guess I don't want to live back in them times no mo', but I sho' seed lots of niggers not doin so well as they did when they was slaves and not havin' nigh as much to eat."[17] Henry Lewis said the slaves knew about the war and talked in the slave quarters about being free, but "we ain't say nothin' where de white folks heared us."[18]

However, not all Texas slaves remembered being aware of the Civil War. Former slave James Hayes indicated that he knew little of the war and that his life was not significantly altered because of it. He did admit that some of the foods they were accustomed to eating were "scarce," but they nonetheless had plenty of food. "But we'uns had plenty to eat and us slaves didn' know what de War was 'bout. I guess we was too ign'rant. De white white folks didn' talk 'bout it 'fore us."[19]

Nonetheless, the suddenness of Robert E. Lee's surrender came as a shock to both Southern whites and blacks. Historian Leon Litwack found many whites in Richmond, Virginia, hid behind locked doors, while the city's newly freed population prayed prayers of thanksgiving, cried tears of joy, and sang songs of jubilation. However, both whites and blacks soon began wondering what their lives would be like without the institution of slavery, and no one could provide an immediate answer.[20]

The defeat of the Confederacy did more than merely end slavery. The defeat of the Confederacy eliminated the idea that individual states could effectively leave the Union. Secondly, it changed the nature of the federal–state relationships, and finally, after nearly a century of debates and compromises, the end of the war *should have* settled the issue of slavery and the place of blacks and the black community as a permanent underclass in this country. Even though historian Alwyn Barr said "Slavery died with the Confederacy," blacks still found it difficult to escape the underclass. Emancipation did not mean an automatic elevation of blacks to an equal social, political, or economic status with whites.[21]

Even though General William T. Sherman issued Field Order No. 15 in August 1865, which allowed eligible black families to inhabit forty-acre lots along the coastal region from Charleston to Florida, the federal government did not have a plan for the relocation of blacks away from the plantation. Field Order No. 15 was not adopted by the government, which meant the black community not only faced uncertainty as they transitioned from free labor to wage-earners, but they also found themselves relegated to refugee status.[22]

Their status as "war refugees" led to the initial creation of the Bureau of Refugees, Freedmen, and Abandoned Lands, otherwise known as the Freedmen's Bureau. The bureau was charged with supporting former black slaves along the South Carolina coast and the lower Mississippi Valley.[23] At the same time, the government faced the serious issue of the readmission of Confederate states, and perhaps more importantly, determining the new relationship of the black community in Southern society in particular, and in the United States in general.[24]

After the assassination of Lincoln, Southerner Andrew Johnson became president and initially spoke and acted like the ruling radicals in Congress. However, within three years these same Radicals would impeach him and come within one vote of removing him from office. Even though he was not ideologically opposed to slavery, he was opposed to the extreme power held by the Southern slave owners. Historian Kenneth Stampp argued that Johnson designed his reconstruction plan to benefit the working class in Southern society, but his ongoing conflicts with the radicals in Congress limited his political agenda and nearly ended his presidency.[25]

However, the radicals took control of the reconstruction process in 1867 and subsequently divided the South into five military districts. The new radical governments were led by Yankee carpetbaggers, many of whom had little or no political experience; scalawags, white Southerners who sided with the carpetbaggers to share in their spoils; and the newly freed blacks, who voted as told. Thus, many Southern whites believed that these new radical governments and carpetbaggers, in particular, were going to change their social, political, and economic structures. To maintain some sense of what they considered the proper order, particularly social order, Southern whites prevented blacks from owning weapons and established racist policies that tried to keep blacks permanently disenfranchised. Furthermore, Southern planters used every legal and illegal maneuver to replace slavery with a form of serfdom designed to keep the black community in social and political subordination to white authority.[26]

Fortunately for the Freedmen's Bureau and Southern blacks, army officer Oliver O. Howard served as commissioner and was a good administrator and sympathetic to the plight of blacks. The same could not be said for some of the other Freedmen's Bureau officers. Complaints sometimes surfaced implicating Freedmen's Bureau officers of "negligent, offensive, and corrupt conduct."[27] Although Howard tried to find local officers who shared his passions, he was often forced to rely on those who were merely carrying out their orders. As a result, W. E. B. DuBois believed the Freedmen's Bureau did not always choose the correct course of action.

> Survey of the conditions and needs in every state and locality; to relieve immediate hunger and distress; to appoint state commissioners and upwards of 900 bureau officials; to put the laborers to work at regular wage; to transport laborers, teachers and officials; to furnish land for the peasant; to open schools; to pay bounties to black soldiers and their families; to establish hospitals and guard health; to administer justice between man and former master; to answer continuous and persistent criticism, North and South, black and white; to find funds to pay for all this.[28]

Arguably the two most important tasks of the Freedmen's Bureau involved the distribution of land and the protection of the former slaves from violence. Unfortunately, it was almost impossible for the Freedmen's Bureau to fully protect blacks. Too often there were no witnesses willing to testify, and as a result most crimes went unpunished. The idea of issuing freed slaves land would have given blacks land and encouraged them to be independent farmers. However, that met intense resistance because it meant the federal government would take land away from the former white slave owners. This led to twentieth-century blacks demanding the federal government to make good on the promise of "40 acres and a mule."[29]

Even though the Freedmen's Bureau failed to achieve many of its national objectives, it was nonetheless an important contribution in expanding the government's limits of paternalism. Sensing the government's willingness to ensure the rights and provide for the well-being of its poor, a coalition of poor farmers and industrial workers appeared on the political scene and made an immediate impact. Although their movement was short-lived, its impact could be seen in the Progressive movement and later in the New Deal.[30]

Many white Texans never accepted the defeat of the Confederacy, believing instead that they merely quit for the benefit of the Union.[31] Many of Texas' former slaves remembered the rebelliousness of some whites after returning home from the war. One slave recalled the following song as an example of the animosity felt by white Texans at the end of the war:

> O, I'm a good old rebel, and dat's jus' what I am,
> And for dis land of freedom, I do not give a damn;
> I'm glad we fought again 'em, and only wish we'd won,
> And I ain't asked no pardon for anything I've done.
>
> I won't be reconstructed, I'm better dan dey am,
> And for a carpetbagger I do not give a damn.
> So I'm off to de frontier, soon as I can go—
> I'll fix me up a wagon and start for Mexico!
>
> I can't get my musket and fight dem now no more,
> But I'm not goin' to love dem, dat an certain sho'—
> I don't want no pardon for what I was or am,
> I won't be reconstructed, and I don't give a damn.[32]

In their examination of the black community after emancipation, historians Leon Litwack and Frank Tannenbaum found that it mattered little if the former slaves left their former masters immediately after emancipation or stayed. This decision was their first exercise of freedom as they began making decisions for

Cato Carter

their lives and that of their families and community.³³ In Texas, the former slaves remembered their various reactions to freedom. Some were overcome with joy and excitement, whereas others were candid in their apprehension of their future as freed people.³⁴

William Adams said, "After de war dere was a lot of excitement 'mong de niggers. Dey was rejoicin' and singin.' Some of 'em looked pussled, sorter skeered like. But dey danced and had a big jamboree."³⁵ Armstead Barrett stated when the slaves first learned of their freedom, "dey all shoutin.'" However, he also remembered in vivid details how some of the whites reacted to these celebrations. Barrett said a female slave was "cut wide 'cross de stomach" by a passing white man because of her excessive celebration. "I didn't git nothin' when us freed. Only some cast-off clothes. Long time after I rents de place on halves and farms most my life."³⁶ Martin Ruffin remembered vividly when he and the other slaves first heard the news that they were free. He described the commotion of uncontrollable relief and happiness, "You ought to see 'em jump and clap their hands and pop them heels."³⁷

Former slave Cato Carter also recalled how some slave owners tearfully announced to their former chattel, "You are free to do as you like, 'cause the damned Yankees done 'creed you are. They ain't a nigger on my place what was born here or ever lived here who can't stay here and work and eat to the end of his days, as long as this old place will raise peas and goobers. Go if you wants, and stay if you wants."³⁸

Many of the oral narratives illustrate the confusion caused by freedom. When told he was free, former slave Daniel Phillips asked his former owner, "Wha' dat mean, Marse Tommy?"³⁹ Phillips had no idea that the Civil War was over or its ultimate consequences. Nonetheless, the idea of freedom was a vague concept. Even as freed individuals, blacks still found it difficult to escape racial oppression and the end of slavery did not automatically ensure social and political equality with whites. Although Republicans ended slavery, they did not always provide a means for the slaves to successfully make the transition from slavery to freedom.[40]

Blacks were not the only ones confused by the suddenness of their emancipation. White Texans openly questioned what would become of their cherished state and many responded with intense hostility when the occupying Union army forced them to release their slaves or pay them for their labor. Former slaves William Mathews, Susan Merritt, and William Thomas remembered the defiance of their former masters when told to release their slaves. Mathews said they kept working well after freedom because their owner, "old Buck Adams," would not let them go. It was not until "de freedom man come and read de paper, and tell us not to work no more 'less us gits pay for it," did Adams release them.[41] Merritt said they were not told they were free for three months. A "Union man" came to the plantation and read the order stating they were free. Nonetheless, she commented that they still were not allowed the option to go or stay. "[M]assa make us work sev'ral months after that. He say we git 20 acres land and a mule but we didn't git it."[42] Like Mathews and Merritt, Thomas also stated they he and his fellow slaves were unaware of emancipation until Union soldiers came through the area and forced slave owners to comply.[43]

Although some slave owners refused to acknowledge the emancipation order, others did acknowledge it but still refused to allow the former slaves to leave the plantation. Former slaves Julia Malone and Walter Rimm detailed the extreme measures some of the former slaves endured to enjoy freedom. Malone said her former owner would not let her leave the plantation even though most of the other slaves were already gone. She further stated that the only way she escaped the plantation was when the woman who raised her literally stole her from her former owner when he and his wife were away. She believed she was forced to remain because it was her responsibility to raise the owner's children.[44] Similarly, Rimm told a story of a young female slave who had to run away from the plantation after freedom because, "Massa Weams won't let her have her freedom. Lots of slaves has to do that."[45]

Although some slave owners did not free their slaves until forced to do so, Annie Row's narrative indicates that some were distraught to the point of death. Born near Rusk, Texas, Row remembered her former slave owner getting a notice two years into the war notifying him of the death of one of his two sons who had joined the Confederate army. She said he immediately turned around and struck her mother with a poker, grabbed his gun, and proceeded to the fields apparently intent on killing as many of his slaves as his grief would allow.

> Him takes de gun offen de rack and starts for de field whar de niggers am a-workin.' My sister and I sees that and we'uns starts runnin' and screamin', 'cause we'uuns has brothers and sisters in the field. But the good Lawd took a hand in that mess and de marster ain't gone far in de field when him draps all of a sudden. De death sets on de marster and de niggers comes runnin' to him. Him can't talk or move and dey tote him in de house.[46]

The next day he was dead. When the other son returned from the war, he informed the slaves that they were free and could stay or go. Row recalled "Mos' of 'em left as soon's dey could." As a result, Row stated that the surviving son later killed himself by cutting his own throat with a razor. A note found next to his body said he didn't want to live, "'cause de nigger free and dey's all broke up."[47]

Former slave Jack Bess recalled that he was definitely glad when freedom came, but he knew he was facing an uncertain future. "[W]e didn' know nothin' to do but jes stay on dere, and we did 'bout three years and de boss pays us a little by de month for our work."[48]

Former slaves Peter Mitchell, Tom Holland, and Will Adams each remembered slaves having to take care of themselves without any help from their former owners. Mitchell said, "When freedom come dey turn us loose and say to look out ourselves. Mos' of de slaves jus' works round for de white folks den and gits pay in food and de clothes, but after while de slaves larns to take care demselves."[49] Holland said his slave owner went to war but never returned, so it was his wife who told them they were free. Without instructions on where to go or what to do, Holland remembered, "So we starts to cry and asks her what we gwine do. She said we could stay and farm with her and work her teams and use her tolls and land and pay her half of what we made, 'sides our supplies. That's a happy bunch of Negroes when she told us this."[50] Adams also stated there were tears on hearing the news that they were free, but like Holland, these were not tears of joy but rather fear. "They's lots of cryin' and weepin' when they sot us free. Lots of them didn't want to be free, 'cause they knowed nothin' and had nowhere to go."[51]

Former slave Charley Mitchell said that he knew of the war (even though whites would not talk about the war in front of their slaves), heard about freedom, but his reminiscences focused on the fact that they were not given the necessary information or resources to be successful as freed individuals. He commented they had to "do the best we could" and he also remembered hearing about possible compensation to the former slaves but to his knowledge he believed no former slave ever received anything. As a result, "We had to go to work for whatever they'd pay us, and we didn't have nothing and no place to go when we was turned loose, but down the street and road."[52] Former slave Thomas Johns also mentioned being promised some form of compensation for slavery. Even though he remained on the plantation until 1874, Johns said, "De Yankees told us niggers when dey freed us after de war dat dey would give each one of us 40 acres of land and a mule. De nearest I'se ever come to dat is de pension of 'leven dollars I gets now. But I'se jus' as thenkful for dat as I can be."[53]

Within all the emotions and confusion of their uncertain future, there were crops that still needed to be tended. Therefore, not knowing where to go, and the white land owners not being offered a substitute labor pool, many of the former slaves stayed on or near the plantation.[54] Former slave Liza Jones said her former owner cried when freedom came because, "times was hard. De white boys, dey go out in de field and work den, and hard work, 'cause dey don't have de slaves no more." Her father decided to stay and work for wages.[55]

Emma Watson told how her family decided to remain with their owners, the Forresters, even though they only gave them food and clothes "but no money."[56] Like Watson, William Paxton stayed on the plantation and received wages until he left in 1867. On leaving the plantation, Paxton joined the army and served with the Twenty-fourth Infantry and fought the American Indians in Texas and throughout the west.[57]

Former slave Alice Houston said her former owner told them they were free but they wanted to stay because they did not know where to go. Most of the slaves remained several more years as sharecroppers.⁵⁸ Likewise, Elsie Reece stated that her former owner read the order giving them their freedom, but he also questioned what they slaves would now do.

> Massa never say 'nother word and works away. De cullud folks say, 'where we'uns gwine live? What we'uns gwine do?' Dey frets all night. Next mornin' massa say, 'What you'uns gwine do?' Uncle John say, 'When does we have to go?' Den massa laughs hearty and say dey can stay for wages or work on halves. . . . Well, sar, dere a bunch of happy cullud folks after dey larnt dey could stay and work, and my folks stays nearly two years after 'mancipation. Den us all move to Navasota and hires out as cooks.

Many of the former slaves *chose* to stay on the plantation and began working for wages. This was perhaps their first exercise of freedom in their lives. However, in time, many began slowly moving away from the plantation and the memories of slavery.⁵⁹ Aunt Pinkie Kelly from Brazoria County admitted to not knowing much about the war, and her owner did not immediately tell his slaves they were free. Although they were happy they soon realized they had nowhere to go. "Law, we sho' shout, young folks and old folks too. But we stay there, no place to go, so we jes stay, but we gits a little pay."⁶⁰ Born in Harrison County, former slave Lizzie Jones also said her former owner did not immediately tell them they were free, but they nonetheless stayed another four years.

Former slave Betty Powers remembers her owner advising the slaves to remain with him on the plantation until they were able to take care of themselves and make their own decisions for their lives. "He 'vises dem to stay till dey git de foothold and larn how to do. Lots stayed and lots go. My folks stays 'bout four years and works on shares." Her father then bought his own land near the plantation.⁶¹ Former slave Lewis Jones remembered his former owner offering to pay those who would stay after freedom. "Some stays and some goes off, but mammy and pappy and me stays. Dey never left dat plantation and I stays 'bout 8 years."⁶² Likewise, former slave Henry Probasco stated that his former owner told them they were free and said they could stay or go. "Yous am free and dem what wants to go, let me know. I'll 'range for de pay or to work de land on shares." Probasco's parents stayed, "but in 'bout a year pappy moves to Waco and run a shoe shop."

Through the summer and winter of 1865, the former slaves began migrating from their plantation to the nearest city or other rural areas.⁶³ Although there were definite instances of black men deserting their slave families, Texas' former slaves also remembered black men who continued to see themselves as husbands and fathers.

Former slaves Lu Perkins and Lu Lee both recited their experiences at emancipation when their slave husbands deserted them. Perkins said her first husband left her and their child and went back to Mississippi after emancipation.⁶⁴ Lee described her husband by saying that he "wasn't much good." Apparently, he sold crops that did not belong to him, which came to the attention of the local authorities. Lee indicated that he eventually left the family.⁶⁵

Sarah Ford

However, former slaves Sarah Ford and Walter Rimm commented that their fathers did not abandon them and each continued his role as husband and father after emancipation. Ford's former owner instructed her father to leave the plantation after emancipation because he was considered a bad influence on the other former slaves. Ford's father complied, but he later returned for his family and they settled near East Columbia. Rimm stated that his mother wanted to stay on the plantation because they had nowhere to go. Undaunted, his father packed up the family and left. Rimm recall that their former owner approached his parents six months after they left and asked to return as sharecroppers. "Den massa tells us we can live on de old place without rent and have what we can make."⁶⁶ They stayed another two years on the plantation, but this time it was their choice.

Like Rimm's father, many former slaves recalled leaving the plantation as soon as possible. Former slave Andy Anderson said he left the plantation as soon as he found out they were free.[67] Susan Ross said after freedom her brother, "whoop, run and jump a high fence and told mammy goodbye. Den he grab me up and hug and kiss me and say, 'brother gone, don't 'spect you ever see ne no more.' I don't know where he go, but I never did se him 'gain."[68]

US history documents that slavery died with the Confederacy in 1865, but for the nearly four million black slaves in this country freedom and equality under the law would not be realized for another one hundred years. They were no longer legally bound to the land of their former master, unless they entered into a labor contract commonly referred to as sharecropping. Unfortunately, many of the newly freed slaves were socially and economically ignorant and found themselves bound to the land with their movements restricted as any time before 1865.

NINE

LIFE AFTER SLAVERY

After the end of the Civil War, many of Texas' former slaves recalled that they received little from their former masters. Those that were allowed to strike out on their own did so with whatever possessions they could carry. However, with freedom came the uncertainties of living in a society that refused to see them as anything other than chattel, and this caused insurmountable obstacles for Texas' black community. Many whites refused to see the black community as having the same rights as whites and established laws, to restrict their movements. Blacks were free, but many still found themselves cheated out of their labor, such as Andrew Goodman's father, and others were subjected to beatings and rape, and continued suffering the degradation associated with being born black and a slave in the United States.[1]

Generally speaking, Texas' white population viewed the agents of the Freedmen's Bureau as an occupying force and not as an agency to help transition blacks from slavery to freedom. The Freedmen's Bureau operated in Texas from September 1865 until July 1870. These five years serve as a perfect case study of government-sponsored paternalism. In Texas, as in other Southern states, the Bureau's primary responsibility was overseeing the transition from slavery to freedom for the state's black population. Crucial to this transition was the establishment of an agriculture system and schools for blacks. However, the men that served as the assistant commissioners in Texas may not have fully supported the idea of black equality because they did not insist that the courts apply the laws regardless of race.[2]

By December 1868 the lack of funds and local support led to the closing of local bureau offices and the cessation of all its programs except those involving

Andrew Goodman

education. Incidentally, education through the establishment and operations of black schools was the one area that the Freedmen's Bureau excelled.³ Even though some whites in Texas tried to educate blacks before emancipation, wholesale attempts at education did not occur until after 1865. Rosina Hoard recalled how her master's son tried to teach slaves to read while they were out in the fields hidden from his father's view. However, the master's arrival meant the end of that day's lessons. "De workers watch for massa and when dey seed him a-ridin' down de hill dey starts singin' out, 'Ole hawg 'round de bench—ole hawg 'round de bench.' Dat the signal and den everybody starts workin' like dey have something after dem."⁴

Nonetheless, blacks began receiving formal lessons after emancipation, and by the end of 1865, more than one thousand blacks were being taught at 16 schools. By 1870, there were 150 schools educating more than nine thousand students in Texas. Although some whites committed savage acts against schools and teachers, these educational programs generally accomplished their goals of educating blacks.⁵

However, there were instances when the Northern white school teachers could not understand the plantation culture of the South. Wayman Williams said that, "Some white school teachers from up North come to teach de chillen, but dey didn't talk like folks here and didn't understan' our talk. Dey didn't know know what us mean when us say 'titty' for sister, and 'budder' for brother, and 'nanny' for mammy."⁶

Although education was their greatest success, protecting the black community was their greatest challenge. The violent acts committed against blacks during the time of the operations of the Freedmen's Bureau in Texas indicated the commitment of some groups and individuals in maintaining white supremacy in Texas. The surviving records from the bureau indicate that many acts of violence committed during the agency's tenure were not random but were, in fact, directed against blacks. From June 1865 to December 1866, there were more than twelve homicides and thirty-nine physical assaults in the Houston area alone.[7]

Correspondence from bureau subassistant commanders to the state assistant commissioners related extreme frustration with the frequency of violence committed in the area and the inability of their offices to prosecute offenders. Black males were often shot and killed. One black male was killed because he did not remove his hat, whereas another was stabbed outside a church because his attacker said he did not get out of the way of a white female. Black females were also brutalized throughout the Houston area as well. One reported being assaulted, stripped, and given two hundred lashes with leather strap because she supposedly made insulting noises when a white female passed her on the street. Another, who was pregnant at the time of her assault, reported receiving 150 blows from the cane of her attacker for no apparent reason. A third stated she was kicked and had her child ripped from her hands. The reason given by the assailant was the woman was taking the child to Houston. Lastly, a black husband and wife were tied, beaten, and kicked because their sons left the plantation without permission. Violence had become so pervasive the bureau officials wondered if any of the offenders would ever be arrested and convicted of their heinous acts.[8]

Ex-slaves Lu Perkins and Bud Jones also witnessed firsthand the racial violence after emancipation and still suffered from their psychological effects at the time of their Depression-era interview. Perkins said she survived the violence of the Klan and prayed for "a wall of the Lord 'round me so they couldn't get at me. The turrible things they did ain't worth tellin'. I wouldn't want to make no recollection of them."[9] Jones indicated that he still remembered blacks hanging from trees, and said, "The Ku Klux was strong in the country. I seen niggers hanging on trees and they cut there ears off."[10]

Some whites in Houston hated the military and the Freedmen's Bureau and believed they were using blacks as a means of punishing Southern whites.[11] There were instances in which whites bragged about the murder of several blacks that worked for the Freedmen's Bureau. These attacks were a barbaric attempt to scare blacks from supporting Northern political efforts.[12] To protect Bureau agents, black and white, local officials requested increased military support as protection and to deter future crimes.[13] Unfortunately, these pleas for support did little to deter the atmosphere of fear and hate that was so pervasive throughout Texas after emancipation.

In addition to random acts of violence, white vigilante groups formed immediately after emancipation, and groups, such as the Ku Klux Klan and the Black Hawks, terrorized blacks.[14] Unfortunately, Union troops proved ineffective in deterring such violent acts. The veil of secrecy surrounding the Ku Klux Klan (KKK) generally rendered radical governments throughout the South helpless to prevent their activities.

The sudden increase of black participation in the political processes throughout the former Confederacy was particularly troubling for members of the KKK and others dedicated to white supremacy. As a result, many blacks that insisted on voting were often run out of town under threats of death to themselves or family members.[15] Surprisingly, ex-slave Will Adams believed white supremacists were not solely responsible for such violence against blacks. He remembered the influence of Northern carpetbaggers who insisted blacks not only vote, but support anything offered by the Republican party, as a show of loyalty to the assassinated Abraham Lincoln. "I 'members when the Ku Klux business starts up. Smart niggers caused that. The carpet-baggers ruint the niggers and the white men couldn't do a thing with them, so they got up the Ku Klux and stirs up the world. Them carpet-baggers come 'round larnin' niggers to sass the white folks what done fed them. . . . Them carpet-baggers starts all the trouble at 'lections in Reconstruction. Niggers didn't know anythin' 'bout politics."[16]

In Texas, the Klan operated loosely throughout the state during Reconstruction and focused on opposing the new Radical governments. They nonetheless terrorized the black community throughout the state.[17] Ex-slave William Hamilton recalled that Klan activity was particularly horrible near Village Creek, Texas, where they terrorized blacks as a means of exerting their power over the newly freed slaves. "It am allus after dark when dey comes to the house and catches the men whups him for nuttin. Dey has de power and it am done for to show dey has de power."[18]

In perhaps the most interesting commentary on the treatment of blacks during the 1930s, former slave Lu Lee compared the KKK and "paddyrollers" to the police of the 1930s. "They [the Klan and paddyrollers] were just as onery and mean as the policemen are now."[19]

Several former slaves discussed their lives after emancipation and found that there was no general consensus as to the initial direction of the black community. Perkins recalled how her first husband left her and their child and went back to Mississippi after emancipation. Her second husband moved the family to Dallas, where she found work in the "red light district" doing laundry. However, he also left the family and then she married George Perkins but described him as "'nother no-good. They ain't no good in men." She had a total of twelve children, but by the Great Depression they were all deceased. "They is all dead and no help coming from dead chilluns."[20]

James Martin

Like Perkins, Lee also had a difficult family life after emancipation. Lee migrated to Raleigh, North Carolina, and married at twenty-one and after some bad marriages, she married Tucker Lee. He "was good and then not much good neither. He ran away with another woman." Lee found work as a midwife and a cook and proudly shared with the interviewer that she was able to save enough money to send her granddaughter to college.[21]

Conversely, some prospered during emancipation. James Martin enlisted in the army, but he could not remember if he was seventeen or eighteen years old and fought the Indians in Texas. He was born in Virginia in 1847 and was a saddler by trade. After his gaining his freedom, Martin moved to Texas and helped bring the first railroads to San Antonio. When asked about his experiences with the railroads, Martin said, "The Southern Pacific in those days only ran to somewhere near Seguin. I was a spiker and worked the whole distance. Then I helped to build the old railroad from Indianola to Cuero and then from Cuero to Corpus Christi." He also described how he participated in driving cattle from San Antonio to the Dakotas. As a ninety-year-old man, Martin did not like how he was being treated in San Antonio. "If I wasn't so old I'd be rollin' right now. This is no place for colored people. The trouble with people here is they don't know how to treat humanity, white or black."[22]

Bud Jones said he married after emancipation and had two children. However, his wife left him. "My wife wan't much good and she didn't save my money. She thought she might as well throw money away as keep it. She ran away to Terrell and married 'nother nigger. Lestways she tuk up with him." Jones remarried but provided little information about the second wife. But he did say that he went to work for the city of Dallas, and at the time of his interview, he was working for the Dallas gas company polishing the city's red street lanterns.[23]

Jack and Rosa Maddox enjoyed an altogether different experience in their marriage. Even though Jack admitted he was not always the husband Rosa deserved, they were married sixty-nine years at the time of the narrative. Jack first met Rosa 1869 in Louisiana while he was working in a sawmill, and "I sho' loved her the first time I seen her." They married the next year, had a baby, and bought a farm. Jack told the interviewer that at that point in his life "everything in the world was fine then." Even though they worked hard to make the land suitable for farming, their ownership of the land was eventually challenged. Jack said that after the death of the man they *thought* they purchased the land from, they found out title to the land was never transferred. Consequently, his children sold the land.[24]

Eventually the Maddoxes worked as tenants on another Louisiana farm but "every year we come out with nothin' but owin' that man money. After three year him and his son fell out and the son come and told me his paw was beatin' me on the books." This particular son then taught Jack how to read, and the next year Jack said they kept "double books." The next year when the owner said he owed them money Jack referred to his books indicating he was one hundred dollars ahead.[25]

Finally, Jack said they moved to Dallas and raised seven children. "Rosa was the best woman and I never wanted to make no swaps. Its never been too cold, never too bad for her to do for me. Course, I ain't allus been so virtuous. I stepped out the middle the road, but Rosa didn't take on none." At this point Rosa addressed the interviewer and said "I guess it's a man's nature to do with women, and I guess they can't go agin' they nature. But I allus been good. But daddy's a right good man. He was good 'nough to me."[26]

The end of the Civil War brought freedom, the right to vote, *and* continued violence. Carpetbaggers enjoyed the political power gained through black support, but did little to protect them outside of the campaign seasons. Blacks were not elevated above the lower rungs of US society and had little economic and social standing.

Likewise, by the 1930s, Jim Crow racism negatively affected the ability of blacks to establish and maintain family and community cohesiveness, much like those faced by blacks during slavery. The first adversity was the depression itself, which affected the earning power of the black family as black unemployment outpaced those of whites. Secondly, the migration of rural blacks to urban centers, North and South, meant the disruption of families through long, and sometimes permanent, separations. Many of those interviewed as part of the WPA's slave narratives indicated that they did not know where their children where because they left in search of work. Lastly, high divorce rates and housing segregation forced blacks into the most undesirable parts of town while restricting access to many municipal services.

Although there were challenges that negatively impacted the black community during both slavery and depression, there were also ways in which the black community managed to survive. During the antebellum years, blacks in Texas focused on strengthening the family and community through family stability and religion. Likewise, blacks also survived the depression by strengthening family and community relationships through its places of entertainment and recreation, religion, and educational achievements. Even though these places were most often segregated, blacks in Texas were able to turn what should have been a degrading experience into a positive one in which the community developed its own standards of social behavior and expectations.

The WPA interviewers who sought out the surviving former slaves found them living in various conditions throughout the state. Some were in decent health, considering their ages; some were living with their children or other relatives, and others were living alone. Some of the former slaves said they wished they were back in slavery because they remembered having food and being taken care of by their former masters, whereas now they were old, hungry, and alone. The New Deal not only provided the black community with a renewed sense of pride with the slaves' narratives but also provided needed services during the Great Depression, such as food and clothes, that were not always forthcoming by private relief agencies. As a result, the activities and programs sponsored by the New Deal provided the black community financial resources and preserved part of the history that could have been lost.

Seventy years after Robert E. Lee surrendered to Ulysses S. Grant, effectively ending the most divisive episode in the United States, Texas' black community found itself free in name only. Blacks were still suffering under the intense scrutiny of Jim Crow racism, which was too often reminiscent of slavery. Franklin D. Roosevelt's New Deal and WPA did provide some relief to blacks throughout Texas, but as the 1930s came to a close, blacks found themselves in a familiar position: hungry, homeless, and struggling to survive. Although Texas' frontier spirit was still evident among the state's white elite, the depression still wreaked havoc on the poor throughout the state. Blacks were especially vulnerable to any economic, social, and political "hiccup" that occurred. For example, black unemployment increased from 4.8 percent in 1930 to 8.8 percent in 1933, whereas white unemployment only rose from 4.2 percent to 5.4 percent in the same period. New technological advancements coupled with the reduction in cotton production forced more than 500,000 people out of rural areas where some owned their own land but where a majority worked as tenant farmers. By 1937, blacks constituted 25 percent of the state's unemployed, while comprising only 14 percent of the total population.[27]

Notwithstanding the influence of Texas' politicians and powerbrokers, unemployment, homelessness, and racism remained devastating social problems during the 1930s. In 1933 more than 105,000 families, or 7.1 percent, were on the state's relief rolls and by 1934 they had increased to nearly 250,000 families, or 13 percent of the general population. Almost every aspect of Texas's economy suffered. Building construction nearly stopped completely, and cotton prices fell from eighteen cents a pound in 1928 to five cents a pound in 1930. Likewise, the oil industry watched helplessly as the price of crude oil also plummeted from sixty cents to five cents a barrel.[28]

Even with shifts in population from the rural countryside to the state's urban centers, many blacks in Texas still found themselves living in rural communities as tenant farmers and sharecroppers. Conditions made farming difficult in the early days of the depression. Black and white farmers suffered and often combined their meager resources to survive. However, by the late 1930s, after the dust storms subsided, farming in north Texas did become profitable again. In relating his childhood during the depression, Eddie Stimpson, Jr., said:

> In the late thirties the dust storms gone, the earth around Collin was rich and the crop was flourishing. Cotton, corn and wheat was making good and the market was good. Crowded families in town began to thin out as the old farm houses that had been empty for several years came to life again with middle age farmer or farm hands. In Collin County most of the blacks come in from South and East Texas. The white farmers and farm hands come from Oklahoma and Kansas. The crops were good enough for this part of Texas to draw people from far and near.[29]

Still, many Texans, whites and minorities alike, were unable to adapt to the sudden unemployment caused by the depression. Just before shooting himself, a distraught Houstonian left a note indicating that the depression had gotten the best of him. He could not find work and felt too "proud" to ask for help from one of the numerous charities in the city. Suicide seemed his only option. "So I see no other course. A land flowing with milk and honey and a first-class mechanic can't make an honest living. I would rather take my chances with a just God than with an unjust humanity."[30]

Unemployed and homeless, thousands of Texans hitchhiked across the state in search of work, while being frequently forced to seek shelter in "abandoned buildings, caves, dugouts, and shanties made of discarded boxes."[31] San Antonian Lonita Gourley was so desperate for employment, she wrote to Roosevelt asking for his assistance in finding employment with the WPA.[32] Yet this was not the experience of large segments of the state's population. In Dallas, for example, such economic contradictions were prominent. There were the neatly manicured lawns of the city's elite who paid "homage to God and educate [their] children in magnificent churches and schools that are second to none in beauty and facilities." Nestled alongside the slums and shantytowns in other parts of the city, the working class lived in slums and shantytowns that put those inhabited by slaves during the antebellum period to shame.[33]

In Texas, as in other states across the country, private organizations initiated relief activities to care for the hungry and homeless. In Houston, for example, the First Presbyterian Church provided meals to more than seventy-five thousand individuals during the winter of 1930.[34] However, the problems associated with racism were evident in their relief activities, which often included the distribution of food, clothes, and sometimes cash and often denied minorities access to their services. As a result of such overt racism, blacks and Hispanics in Houston were frequently told not to apply for relief services because there was not enough money to take care of the city's white families.[35] Texas' depression-era racism occurred when Governor James V. Allred requested additional funds to increase the number of Civilian Conservation Corps (CCC) camps. Unfortunately, many Texans vocally expressed rabid opposition to any new CCC facilities that might possibly become predominately "Negro" camps, even though the existing CCC facilities were already racially segregated.[36]

Therefore, it was not surprising that blacks and Hispanics experienced the hardships of the depression to a greater degree than most whites. Although white families also experienced the despair of homeless and poverty, the state unemployment rate for blacks was twice that of their white contemporaries.[37] Meanwhile, Texas' Hispanic community also experienced hardships during the 1930s, but there was no significant change from the post-Reconstruction era when they struggled for recognition and survival in Texas' changing economy.[38]

Additionally, the high levels of economic disenfranchisement led to high instances of crime and violence. In a study of black high school graduates in 1933, 31 percent had no real career or educational plans after high school.[39] Violence has always been a part of the urban black community, and Houston's urban communities were no different. By the 1940s and 1950s, the Fifth Ward became known as the "the Bloody Fifth" because of the frequent violent confrontations in the community.[40]

Even with the support of Texas politicians Jesse Jones and John Nance Garner, who ensured that millions of relief dollars flowed into the Lone Star state, it was the activities of the WPA in cities throughout the state that made the real difference for the downtrodden, both black and white. The WPA's operations division sponsored construction-related projects that provided jobs for thousands of blue-collar workers in nearly every community throughout the state. For example, in 1935, its first year of existence in Bexar County, the WPA's operations division sponsored fifty-four projects, the majority of which directly benefited the city of San Antonio, pumping more than one million dollars into the city's economy through employee wages.[41]

San Antonio's public education system also benefited immensely from WPA largesse because the agency built more than $1.2 million in school facilities between 1935 and 1940.[42] Additionally, local sponsors contributed 26 percent of the total funds that led to the construction of schools, two athletic stadiums, and landscaping improvements. An article in the *San Antonio Light* reported that, "the WPA has spent many thousands of dollars more in the county since 1935 in the operation of service projects and lately has contributed to the education of skilled workers under the national defense program."[43]

These types of construction projects were typical throughout Texas. Although some of these projects were small, they filled a definite community need, especially in poor, minority-dominated communities, whose infrastructures and public facilities would have deteriorated further had it not been for the WPA. For example, thanks to WPA funds, blacks in the town of McKinney built a 30' × 35' building to be used as a school for 225 of its children.[44] In another instance, Dallas's black Oak Cliff community was able to remodel its segregated playground for use a community center with WPA funds. Although the operations division focused on manual work, the state's community services projects (classified into three broad categories: Welfare, Community Services, and Research and Records) gave white-collar workers the unprecedented opportunity to positively impact the lives of Texans.[45]

Often those that received food supplies wrote district officials to express their gratitude. Lula Estelle and Lela Buggs, both of Marshall, said their families would have died of starvation had not been for the surplus commodity project. Helen Riggins, also of Marshall, said, "Lord have mercy. Do I get all this many groceries? I do not ever remember having all this many groceries in my kitchen before. This is shore something for us old niggers to be proud of I shore do thank you."[46] Likewise, Isaac Harper stated, "I just don't know what I would do if I did not get these groceries down here. I can tell you right now I appreciate what you all does for me."[47] Emma Moore of Waskom said, "I shore am glad to get these things. I likes it all. I'm not hard to please for I can't work anymore. I have to depend on the good white people, I thank you."[48] Finally, the District 16 commodities project provided meals for 2,285 school children and 3,920 indigent families.[49]

The sewing project in Gilmer produced clothing for the State Colored Orphanage. In her letter to Virginia Chapman, Dorothy Wentland reported that the women of the project "have taken an interest in making the garments for these little Negro children."[50] She concluded her letter by commenting that not only did black children benefit, but also poor children of all races received clothing that was considered "excellent quality."[51]

Providing quality care for infant children was a concern for working parents. As a result, the WPA established nursery programs in practically every community throughout the state. Although many of the nurseries were racially segregated, they were still welcomed in their community by parents with little or no other childcare options. In San Antonio, there were two units of nursery schools in operation: one for Mexican children and the other for black children. Each unit had an average enrollment of forty.[52]

However, because of the racist atmosphere in San Antonio during the depression, those assigned to minority nursery programs were not provided the same opportunities for professional development as those majority nursery programs. Workers at the white nursery school programs had the opportunity to attend training conferences where they learned the WPA policies and how to lead WPA projects. Those assigned to the colored schools only received training in crafts and other job-related skills.[53]

Local black social and religious groups gladly sponsored "negro" nursery schools throughout the state. Although their sponsorship was financially low during the summer months, donations from groups like the Negro Baptist Minister's Association and the Negro Physicians Association provided needed monetary support for those minority nursery schools in San Antonio.

Furthermore, the Negro Baptist Minister's Association in San Antonio led the community in the development of an advisory board for the Negro nursery school.[54] The white Missionary Societies in Gainesville collected and sold used magazines and newspapers for the support and maintenance of that community's black nursery school. Additionally, the wife of the local school principal in Gainesville visited the black nursery school and commented that the project was an asset to the community, as well as to the "Negro race."[55]

The WPA also established a Negro nursery school in Forth Worth that was conveniently located across the street from the Negro public school. To address the health needs of the children, the city's "Negro health nurse" visited the nursery each week. Even though there were established segregated nursery schools throughout the state, records indicated that there was still need for more Negro nursery schools.

Statewide black religious leaders were extremely vocal in petitioning the WPA for the establishment of nursery schools that were convenient to their communities. The Reverend Marvin Robinson, of the Polly Chapel Baptist Church in Texarkana, and Reverend Rector, Pastor of San Antonio's West End Baptist Church, wanted to establish Negro nursery schools in their local communities. In Houston, the Pastor of Fifth Ward's Pleasant Hill Baptist Church, Reverend L. H. Simpson, also wanted a nursery for the predominantly black Fifth Ward after more than two hundred parents attended parent education classes.[56]

Recognizing the need for increased education and training as a means of increasing employment opportunities, the WPA aggressively established adult education centers in as many communities as they could find qualified teachers. Even where there were teachers they often underwent two weeks of training and were then placed under the supervision of trained teachers. In District 7, for example, teachers trained at North Texas State Teacher's College, whereas in District 1, the adult education project established cooperative relationships between the WPA and the Stephen F. Austin State Teacher's College, which allowed the Red Bayou School to establish classes in Bowie County. In the black segregated programs, the district established cooperative agreements between Prairie View A&M College and Gethsemane Negro School.

Segregation played a role in the training of 136 adult education workers in District 4. The district's white teachers received training three hours per day, five days per week. Likewise, the training for blacks followed a similar schedule, but there were differences. Data indicated that, "except that a few hours weekly were assigned to be done in the Negro branch of the City library. This work is carefully supervised, as are the hours of study in the workshop."[57] The supervisors in District 4 seemingly supported segregated programs when they recommended assigning three black teachers to the Rockwall County project to work with the predominantly black programs there. Rockwall had the highest percentage of "illiterate Negroes than any other County in the state" and they felt that only black teachers might be successful there.[58]

In San Antonio, where the training was also segregated, teachers were divided into three groups, two for whites and one for blacks. Adult education programs operated at forty-one schools, churches, and other community centers in the greater San Antonio area. Men and women received elementary school, vocational, and Americanization training. Many in these classes were foreign born, whereas others were native Texans who never had the opportunity to acquire even a grammar school education. By the spring of 1940, eighty-seven teachers were employed in San Antonio and taught literacy, general education, and vocational classes to more than 2,600 individuals. Between March and November 1940, slightly more than 6,000 students received some form of instruction, in addition to conducting thirty-two parent education meetings with nearly 2,500 in total attendance.[59]

District 7 also conducted classes for foreign-born adults in addition to their literacy classes for blacks. General education classes specifically designed for Hispanic were held in Eastland, Fort Worth, and Cisco, plus a library class in Fort Griffin for whites. Along the border district officials reported numerous problems with the Hispanic adult education programs. In Overton, District 1 officials established four new adult education classes in November 1940. However, these adult education classes were segregated: two specified for white children, and the other two for black children.

One of the black workers in District 10, James Valentine, resigned from the adult education program in San Antonio to become the pastor of a church in Athens, Texas. In his letter of resignation, Valentine thanked the WPA and the adult education program for providing him employment that helped him keep his home and put his daughter through college (Prairie View). Finally, Valentine stated "greatest of all, it [working with the WPA] gave me a chance to pursue my course of study and further prepare myself for the position as Pastor of one of our leading churches. I leave with regret, but shall ever do all I can do to further Adult Education and lift up my people."[60]

One of the often overlooked aspects of the slave narratives is the glimpse of what life was like for elderly blacks during the 1930s. The former slaves commented on their marriages, children, and the work they had done since emancipation. However, a constant theme frequently found in the narratives was that of the perceptions of the younger generations growing up in the 1930s. Some of the former slaves were disappointed by the behaviors of the younger people, whereas others expressed intense anger and the obvious disrespect of the hard lives experienced by those who survived slavery.

Certainly the Great Depression was a devastating time for the elderly, especially the black elderly. The generation of elderly blacks was once slaves, and many remembered the slave owner taking care of the elderly slaves who were no longer productive in the fields. Such was not the case in the 1930s. The slave owner was gone, and often so too were the children and other family members.

Imagine being old and alone in the worst financial crisis in the nation's history. It may then be no surprise that many of the former slaves told their WPA interviewer that their lives were better off as slaves.[61] Likewise, former slave Aaron Russell admitted that sometimes he wished he could return to his former slave owner believing that he would be taken care of and fed. Russell was alone and frequently without food. "Times lately I's wish I's back wit de mass, 'cause I has plenty rations dere. It hard to be hungry and dat I's been many times lately."[62]

The former slaves still vividly remembered that the slaves' lives were ones of drudgery and pain, even if the younger generation seemed oblivious to it. Former slave Diane Watson commented that the new generation of blacks had little appreciation, nor understanding, of the horrors of slavery. "If niggers of these days done see what I seed in slavery time they'd pray and thank Gawd every day . . . I tells the young race iffen they come up like me they wouldn't act so smart. They needs somebody to take the smartness outten them."[63]

Like Watson, former slave Willis Winn was also disappointed by the lack of progress blacks had made since emancipation.

> I allus say the cullud race started off wrong when they was freed and is still wrong today. They had a shot to be well off, but they can't keep money. You give one a bank of money and he'll be busted tomorrow. I tells young niggers every day they ought to come down where they'll have some sense. I serves the Lord at home and don't meddle with 'em.[64]

Unfortunately, former slave John McCoy was not disappointed, but angry. McCoy believed slavery was better than freedom because somewhere along the way the black community ceased being a place that cared about one another. "Slave times was de best, 'cause cullud folks am ig'rent and ain't got no sense and in slave times white folks show dem de right way. Now dey is free, dey gits uppity and sassy. Some dese young bucks ought to git dere heads whipped down. Dat larn dem manners."[65] Perhaps the disenchantment with the younger generation of the 1930s is best summed up by former slave Bert Strong, who shared with his WPA interviewer, "Mos' the young niggers am gwine to Hell. They don't 'preciate things. They has lots more'n we ever did. They can go to school and all, but they don't 'preciate it."[66]

Unfortunately, the scars of slavery were not always physical; sometimes they were emotional and mental as well. Former slave Rose Williams shared with her WPA interviewer that she was put on the auction block at fifteen years old and remembered being described as a "portly, strong young wench. She's never been 'bused and will make de good breeder." As if being auctioned like livestock was not enough to alter one's mental and emotional state, Williams found herself "placed" with a man she did not love for the purpose of rearing children.

> Dere am one thing Massa Hawkins does to me what I can't shunt from my mind. I knows he don't do it for meanness, but I allus holds it 'gainst him. What he done am force me to live with dat nigger Rufus, 'gainst my wants.... [After refusing to be intimate] Woman, I's pay big money for you and I's done that for de 'cause I wants you to raise me chillens. I's put you to live with Rufus for dat purpose. Now, if you doesn't want whippin' at de stake, yous do what I wants.... So I 'cides to do as de massa wish and so I yields."[67]

Williams may have eventually acquiesced to her new owner's wishes, but decades later she still resented him and it no doubt affected her life and other relationships.

In hindsight, the transition from slavery to freedom was a difficult one for most of the former slaves, but the New Deal's WPA project gave them the opportunity to share their recollections of their time in bondage, the difficulty associated with transitioning into a free society, and their living conditions in the 1930s. For some of the former slaves, their living conditions in the 1930s were too reminiscent of their former slave quarters. For instance, former slave Louis Love told his interviewer, "Us live in shacks 'bout like dese 'round here."[68]

Even though the WPA projects were introduced to provide employment, many of their products made lasting contributions to our society and our understanding of history. Specifically the interviewing of former slaves provided insights into perhaps the most abhorrent time in US history. The stories told by the survivors of slavery convey the emotions of happiness when they were able to marry the ones they loved, but also anger, at the incessant punishment endured by many at the hands of sadistic owners and overseers. Additionally, these same stories also provided a seldom seen glimpse into the existence of elderly blacks during the Great Depression. Granted, a majority of Americans suffered through the widespread economic crises that gripped the world in the 1930s, but the WPA captured the lives of those who openly questioned if living on the plantation was preferred to being old and living alone. In the end, the WPA made contributions to our understanding of two of the most turbulent times in US history.

TEN

CHANGING SLAVERY'S PARADIGM

Slavery and institutionalized racism through Jim Crow left the black community in Texas, and generally throughout the country, in disarray by the 1930s. However, the New Deal inadvertently interjected a new sense of pride into the black community through the stories of former slaves. The adversities they witnessed and survived serve as proof that the soul cannot be restricted by physical restraints. The Slaves Narratives Project led to a general reinterpretation in the study of slavery and the acceptance of the records left by the slaves as legitimate.

What follows is what historians call a historiographical essay. The purpose is to discuss some of the traditional and "must-read" secondary sources that the general reader may want to delve into if he or she would like further information about the topics previously discussed in this book. I include it here not to appease historians but to encourage others to seek out those works that illustrate the challenges faced by the black community since 1865. The black community has a rich history in this country. Unfortunately, that history is too often told by historians who have little understanding of what life was and is still like for those of the darker hue living under the ever-present fear of racism.

When Franklin D. Roosevelt became president in 1932, he promised a "New Deal" for all Americans. However, as he neared the end of his first term, Roosevelt found the New Deal produced many successes but not enough to end the social and economic crises caused by the Great Depression. In an effort to secure his reelection and provide relief to the millions that were suffering across the nation, Roosevelt led the US Seventy-Fourth Congress in appropriating funds for the establishment of the Works Progress Administration (WPA) in April 1935. The WPA established relief projects that provided meaningful work to the thousands of unemployed throughout the country. Many of these projects, especially those associated with community services, not only provided employment, but also simultaneously preserved US culture. For example, one such project, the Slave Narratives, interviewed, photographed, and recorded thousands of former slaves as they recalled their experiences as slaves in the "Land of the Free."[1]

There is little doubt that the institution of slavery holds a unique place in US history. Many nineteenth-century slave owners argued that slavery was a civilizing process for the African "heathens," whereas others justified slavery by misinterpreting the Bible. However, the first widely publicized argument against slavery appeared in Harriet Beecher Stowe's novel *Uncle Tom's Cabin*. Stowe was the daughter of a New England clergyman and was active in abolitionist propaganda. Appearing in 1852, *Uncle Tom's Cabin* was an indictment against slavery, not Southerners. Still, her depictions of the plantation as a place of unspeakable horrors, where slave owners and overseers were abusive taskmasters and the slave were the poor downtrodden victims, resulted in a wide range of responses. For abolitionists, it was proof that the institution of slavery was contrary to the principals on which this country was founded. To the plantation aristocracy, this was an indication that the North intended to alter their way of life by somehow changing slavery.

The history of the United States as presented in the late nineteenth century depicted slavery as fundamentally evil and a burden to the slave owner and a moral wrong inflicted on the hapless and defenseless slave. In fact, abolitionists continually focused on the wretched conditions of the black slave, who incidentally had few rights in US society that white men were obliged to respect. This view of history certainly focused on the dominance of the slave owner because he was free to work his slaves from the earliest rooster crow in the mornings to well past sundown. Slave historiography also indicates that this particular class of "Southern Gentlemen" seldom hesitated in rampant sexual activities with female slaves, as exhibited in the numbers of slave children fathered by their mothers' owners, much to the consternation of his all-too-aware wife. However, this version of history also indicted the North as well as the South because the North allowed the system to gain an early foothold in this country.[2]

The abolitionist version of slavery was also evident in Albert Bushnell Hart's 1906 study of slavery, *Slavery and Abolition*. As the son and grandson of nineteenth-century abolitionists, Hart saw slavery as disastrous to both Southern blacks and whites and prevented both from moving into the rapidly increasing technological age of the twentieth century.[3] There were few objections to this abolitionist history, in part because Southerners were embracing the mantra of the New South as a place of industrial progress. As such, they wanted to separate themselves from the old ways of their fathers and embrace a new future by putting loss of the Civil War as far behind them as possible.[4]

Nearing the close of the First World War, Ulrich B. Phillips presented his revision of the abolitionist doctrine. His *American Negro Slavery* rested on the premise that blacks were inherently inferior to whites and that the plantation system was not harsh or cruel but was in fact a necessary civilizing process that prepared blacks for the responsibility of citizenship in this country.[5] This view coincided with the resurgence of the Ku Klux Klan and the atrocities suffered by blacks throughout the country. The result was a Southern racist view of history that was accepted throughout the country.[6]

The next revisionist history challenged Phillips' theories. Richard Hofstadter questioned the applicability of many of Phillips' conclusions because they were based on a limited sample of plantation records. Hofstadter and others argued that such a limited sample could not satisfactorily support the racist Southern histories being written. Therefore, Hofstadter challenged the methods but made sure he stayed away from any semblance of a personal attack against Phillips.[7]

Herbert Aptheker and Stanley Elkins also challenged Phillips' belief that the Southern plantation was a civilizing structure beneficial to the so-called "black savages." Aptheker's *American Negro Slave Revolts* presented slavery as a ghastly atmosphere in which blacks were beaten, sold, and terrified at the whims of whites and that there were hundreds of slave revolts, even though most were relatively unsuccessful.[8] Elkins agreed that slavery was brutal, but he also argued that *any* oppressive environment reduced its victims to the infantile state of childlike behavior and that such behavior was not contingent on race or ethnicity. He focused on the actions and attitudes of the slave field hands and created perhaps the most enduring legacy of his seminal work, *Slavery: A Problem in American Institutional and Intellectual Life*, that being the caricature of Sambo. Whereas Aptheker argued that rebelliousness among slaves was commonplace, and in fact a dominant characteristic of the US slave, Elkins believed slaves enjoyed the paternal affections of the owner. Therefore, the personality of the Sambo as simple minded, lazy, and seeking the unabashed approval of whites quickly became entrenched in Southern lore during the 1950s as Southerners fought to maintain the existing caste system and the burgeoning black protest movements were threatening. Elkins used the following to describe the Sambo characteristics.

> Sambo, the typical plantation slave, was docile but irresponsible, loyal but lazy, humble but chronically given to lying and stealing; his behavior was full of infantile silliness and his talk inflated with childish exaggeration. His relationship with his master was one of utter dependence and childlike attachment; it was indeed this childlike quality that was the very key to his being.[9]

This caricature found a welcoming audience in the 1950s and became the typical standard for the portrayal of blacks throughout the country. Elkins adequately supported his assumptions that these childlike Sambo characteristics were the result of the oppressive plantation system, as he deftly compared the oppressiveness of the plantation with the Nazi concentration camps. However, the Sambo persona was attached solely to black slaves in this country.

Like Elkins, Kenneth Stampp, whose *The Peculiar Institution* became the new standard in slavery studies when published in 1956, attacked Phillips' racist assertions that the plantation was an unprofitable, benign paternalistic community.[10] Methodologically, Stampp's sample of plantation records was broader than Phillips' was, and, like Aptheker and Elkins, saw the plantation as a totalitarian system in which the masters ruled and the slaves were unable to create any resemblance of culture and identity.[11]

There is little doubt that the civil rights movement of the 1950s influenced Stampp, whose view of plantation life curiously mirrored the prevailing image of the Jim Crow era where blacks, like their slave counterparts, appeared to have minimal cultural identity. Racially, Stampp argued that there was never reliable data indicating blacks were satisfied being slaves under the supposed loving care of their white owners, and any such assumptions were based on the mistaken belief that blacks were racially inferiority as accepted by Phillips and William Dunning.[12] Nonetheless, the study of slavery reached a turning point. From this point forward all evaluations and reevaluations of slavery would no longer use Phillips' opinion that blacks were inherently inferior to whites as their point of departure. Instead, future studies involving slavery reconsidered Stampp and Elkin's premise that black slaves were not biologically inferior, but they were incapable of creating a viable culture because of the brutality of slavery.[13]

Slave studies soon took a drastic new turn in the late 1960s with the acceptance of slave narratives as a viable historical resource. Amid social turmoil over black civil rights and the Vietnam War, historians began mining every available source documenting black culture. Historians were already aware of slave narratives, but they held serious reservations over their accuracy and academic applicability.

Nonetheless, it was the students at Fisk University who were the first to interview ex-slaves in 1929 while a similar project at Southern University resulted in the 1935 article by John Cade, "Out of the Mouths of Ex-Slaves."[14] Cade presented the value of these oral interviews as primary sources in evaluating slavery and plantation life as seen by the oppressed (slave). Cade understood the Phillips-influenced history that portrayed blacks as racially inferior to whites and saw these oral interviews as the vehicle for changing that paradigm:.

> After all the story of Negro life must be told—whether by white or by black or by both. At present, both are at work. From the pens of whites, we may get reflections of ideas and attitudes impossible from Negro authors. From the persons of the other race, when they are frank and loyal to the truth, Negroes are able to find out just what is on the minds of their white neighbors. The Negroes may thus understand the basis of the white people's reaction to the blacks about them even though they may not agree with them as to attitudes. One can thereby trace lines of thought as the actually develop. Likewise, black authors may interpret their people to the world more faithfully than white authors. They are able to set forth the real black man as he was, is, and hopes to be. The one interpretation may counterbalance the other.[15]

For the first time former slaves discussed their familial relationships, the clothes they wore, and the food they ate; their relationships with whites; and the expectations of work on the plantation. However, the Great Depression still dominated virtually every aspect of US life and the questions of whether or not blacks were physically and mentally inferior took a back seat to questions of providing food and shelter to the needy, both black and white.

Encouraged by the civil rights movement, a new generation of historians in the 1960s began reconsidering the usefulness of the Federal Writers Project's Slave Narratives as primary sources in examining black slaves and slavery. This reconsideration began with Norman Yetman's "Background of the Slave Narrative Collection" which argued that the previously held stereotype of the contented slave was contradicted by the narratives that told of numerous rebellions and attempted escapes. Although Yetman opened the door for a reassessment of the slaves' narratives, it was George Rawick's *The American Slave: A Composite Autobiography* that completely challenged all previously held beliefs about slavery, especially the supposed docility of blacks.[16]

Several studies soon appeared taking exception to Elkins' Sambo assumptions by mining the extensive volumes of slaves' narratives. The works of John Blassingame, Paul Escott, Eugene Genovese, Herbert Gutman, Gladys-Marie Fry, Charles Joyner, Deborah Gray White, Leon Litwack, and Philip Foner relied heavily on the narratives to refute not only Elkins but also Phillips. Of the aforementioned authors, only Blassingame's *The Slave Community* uses the autobiographies of blacks from the nineteenth century instead of the slave narratives of the 1920s and 1930s. Through these autobiographies Blassingame found that blacks were not docile Sambos; however, they were far from being radical insurgents as well. The second edition of *The Slave Community* included new information not discussed in the first printing such as religion, which Blassingame argues played a significant role in the indoctrination process before and after emancipation.[17]

Escott's *Slavery Remembered* used the narratives but he applied a scientific methodology hoping to quantify the narratives by race of the interviewer and race of the interview subject, among other factors. His findings showed that black behavior during slavery were fairly consistent with their disposition after emancipation. Although there were instances of the Sambo mentality, Escott believed it was the exception, not the norm.[18]

Like Escott, Gutman's *The Black Family in Slavery and Freedom* used scientific methods to examine the black family and found blacks were able to establish family kinship ties, even when husbands lived in nearby plantations. Furthermore, he argued that blacks developed a viable culture that defined its own parameters during slavery and emancipation. The ability to socially and culturally adapt belies Elkins' childlike aberration.[19]

The ability to adapt is also prominent in Gladys-Marie Fry's *Night Riders in Black Folk History*. Through her examination of the slave narratives, Fry concluded that blacks were a valuable economic resource, and as such, the white South tried to maintain control through the use of fear (superstitions) and violence. The idea of superstitions and violence as control methods is what eventually led the Ku Klux Klan to don the white custom in an effort to look like some kind of ghost or other supernatural being. Fry found the slaves developed their own culture on the plantation that functioned to preserve their own sense of identity, provide meaningful relationships, and protect them from excess white violence. She further argued that Elkins' Sambo caricature was merely a black ruse to convince whites that their "supernatural" form of control was working, when in fact it was not.[20]

The slaves' unique culture and institutions were identified in a case study of slaves in All Saints Parish, a community in South Carolina, in Charles Joyner's *Down by the Riverside: A South Carolina Slave Community*. Joyner used the slave narratives to identify how the slaves developed their own folktales and language, in addition to their perceptions of food, clothing, religion, and leisure. He also illustrated how black slaves melded African traditions with the cultures developed on the plantations to create a distinctive black identity.[21]

Thankfully, the slaves' narratives included the voices of black women as well as those of black men. The experiences of black women were explored in-depth *in Ar'n't I A Woman? Female Slaves in the Plantation South* by Deborah Gray White. White argued that during slavery black women suffered under the double burden of being black *and* female. The narratives also allowed White to explore the two popular myths held concerning black women of the antebellum period: that of the jezebel and the mammy. She found that the wanton Jezebel was a white manufactured image to justify rape and other sexual misconducts. The mammy, typically described as an overweight asexual person, was believed to have freely moved throughout the "big house." However, White believed the mammy was carefully supervised by the white mistress of the house and seldom operated independently.[22]

Finally, the creation of stable family units after emancipation was the subject of Leon Litwack's *Been in the Storm So Long*. Litwack specifically examined former slaves and the complexities of the emancipation process. He found that former slaves exhibited a variety of reactions, some optimistic and others disappointment, as they adjusted to freedom after generations as chattel slaves. Litwack's extensive use of the narratives allowed the former slaves to tell their own stories with minimal interpretation.[23]

Whereas Litwack focused on the former slaves and their transition to freedom, historian Stephanie Shaw argued that the slaves' narratives are valuable primary sources for the examination of blacks in both slavery *and* the Great Depression. She clearly demonstrated that the narratives address many questions central to understanding blacks during the 1930s, including the Great Migration and familial relationships.[24]

Several studies used the Texas Slave Narratives in examining slavery and freedom in Texas. In 1974, Ron Tyler and Lawrence Murphy edited the *Slave Narratives of Texas*, a volume of selected narratives illustrating the depth of the WPA project in Texas. Although the authors focused on the nature of slavery as seen through the narratives, it is Tyler's introduction on slavery in Texas that sets this manuscript apart from those that followed. He deftly discussed the history of slavery in Texas from the Austin's first colonies in the 1820s to Granger's General Order No. 3 in 1865. Along the way he discussed the complexities of slavery and its eventual positive relationship to Texas' economy. In fact, Tyler found that Texans acquiesced slavery's existence because of the economic necessities coupled with the racist belief that blacks could not function in society without white oversight. Even though Tyler questioned whether or not slavery in Texas was characteristically similar to slavery throughout the old Confederacy, there was no question that slavery was the economic, social, and political foundation in the antebellum South.[25]

Randolph Campbell's *An Empire for Slavery: The Peculiar Institution in Texas, 1821–1865* provides the best statewide study of slavery. His analysis balances sources from slave owners and the former slaves to recreate Texas from the initial arrival of US settlers to the "day of jubilee," June 19, 1865, and concluded that slavery in Texas was far from a unique place and was similar to that found in other slave states.[26] Studies by James Smallwood and Merline Pitre examined the experiences of blacks in Texas during their initial years of freedom. Their findings generally indicated that blacks enjoyed their newfound freedom, even if they faced an uncertain future politically and socially.[27]

During the Great Depression, as in slavery, blacks faced varying degrees of adversities that caused many former slaves to fondly remember slavery as a time when someone else was responsible for their care. Historian Nancy Weiss found that the declining living conditions of blacks during the late 1920s and early 1930s was a result of political neglect by the Republican Party. As a result, she contends that the black electorate embraced Roosevelt and the Democrats in 1936 hoping the New Deal would improve their lives.[28] Although numerous studies specifically examined the living conditions of blacks during this time period, they generally found that blacks were socially and politically ostracized and economically restricted to the lowest paying jobs.[29]

Unfortunately, the living conditions of blacks in Texas during the 1930s mirrored those of blacks elsewhere in the country. Several studies examined their social, political, and economic experiences and generally found that blacks lived in segregated communities, were prevented from full political participation because of the white primary system, and limited from accessing many New Deal programs. Overall, these works illustrate the extent to which blacks in Texas fought to attain the elusive rights granted to them after the end of slavery, but not yet realized by the Great Depression.[30]

Although society continues to grapple with the lingering effects of slavery, the New Deal and the WPA preserved the words and voices of those who are often forgotten in mordern debates: those who were enslaved. The interviews conducted as part of the WPA provide every successive generation tangible evidence that they not only existed and survived slavery, but that they also made contributions to the nation's continued development in the nineteenth and twentieth centuries. Thankfully, society now recognizes the legitimacy of the narratives after initially dismissing them as fanciful stories manipulated by the foes of the South.

NOTES

Chapter One
1. For more information on the FWP, see Jerre Mangione, *The Dream and the Deal*.
2. Fisk University Social Science Institute, *Unwritten History of Slavery*.
3. Cade, "Out of the Mouths of Ex-Slaves," 295.
4. Ibid., 294.
5. See Billington, "Government and the Arts"; Larson, "The Cultural Projects of the WPA"; Rose, *Put to Work*.
6. Federal Writers' Project, The Library of Congress Project, Work Projects Administration (District of Columbia), Slave Narratives: a Folk History of Slavery in the United States from Interviews with Former Slaves. http://memory.loc.gov/cgi-bin/ampage?collId=mesn&fileName=001/mesn001.db&recNum=0. (accessed February 1, 2008).
7. Ibid.
8. Blassingame, "Using the Testimony of Ex-Slave," 483.
9. Mazique Sanco, *Slave Narratives*. The dialect referred to was probably the speech patterns of southern blacks. However, since emancipation Sanco worked with the US Army's Tenth Calvary and traveled throughout the Midwest and Mexico. Such exposure probably eliminated the speech patterns normally found in blacks in Texas during the 1930s.
10. Blassingame, "Using the Testimony of Ex-Slave," 483.
11. Susan Ross, *Slave Narratives*.
12. Willis Anderson, *Slave Narratives*.
13. Campbell, *An Empire for Slavery*, 257. The fact that many whites came to Texas with their slaves supports Campbell's assertion that slavery in Texas was not fundamentally different from slavery anywhere else in the United States. "Slavery in Texas did not differ in any fundamental way from the institution as it existed elsewhere in the United States. Claims that somehow Negro bondage was milder or worse in the Lone Star state are morally pointless and historically inaccurate."
14. Stampp, "Rebels and Sambos," 367–368.
15. Blassingame, "Using the Testimony of Ex-Slave," 474.
16. Ibid., 483–486.
17. Josephine Ryles, *Slave Narratives*.
18. James Smith, *Slave Narratives*.
19. Patsy Moses, *Slave Narratives*; Walter Leggett, *Slave Narratives*.

20. Abram Sells, *Slave Narratives*.
21. Henry Lewis, *Slave Narratives*.
22. Callie Shepard, *Slave Narratives*.
23. Mandy Marrow, *Slave Narratives*.
24. Douglass, *Narrative of the Life of Frederick Douglass*, 62.
25. Julia Blanks, *Slave Narratives*.
26. Wes Brady, *Slave Narratives*.
27. Martin Jackson, *Slave Narratives*.
28. Ibid.
29. Millie Manuel, *Slave Narratives*.
30. Felix Haywood, *Slave Narratives*.
31. In the original 1937 interview, his name was spelled "McRay."
32. In addition to Lomax, other notable interviewers of former slaves in the 1940s included John H. Faulk and Charles S. Johnson. A protégé of J. Frank Dobie and Walter P. Webb, Faulk made the folk recordings in Texas during the time he taught English at the University of Texas. In 1941, as part of a collaborative effort between Fisk University and the Library of Congress, Johnson made his folk recordings of former slaves then living in Mississippi.
33. Botkin, *Lay My Burden Down*; Yetman, "The Background of the Slave Narrative Collection," 534–553; Rawick, *The American Slave*.

Chapter Two

1. Miliatos, *Some Aspects of Slavery and Slave Care in Texas*, 10–11. Taylor, *Negro Slavery in Louisiana*, 4. Whites generally believed blacks were better suited to agricultural labor. For a complete examination of the nature of the slave's work, religion, racial attitudes, and its role in the development of Texas as an independent republic, see Campbell's *An Empire for Slavery*.
2. Campbell, *An Empire for Slavery*, 10–12; Richardson, Anderson, Wintz, and Wallace (2001), *Texas*, 49–50, 56–72; Ron Tyler and Lawrence R. Murphy, *The Slave Narratives of Texas* (Austin: Encino Press, 1974), xvii–xxii. Stationed near Galveston, the pirate Jean Lafitte terrorized ships in the Gulf of Mexico and confiscated anything of value. For years he sold slaves to the labor-hunger planters of Louisiana. Campbell related how the famous Jim Bowie and his brothers purchased slaves from Lafitte and transported them to Louisiana for eventual sale throughout the remainder of the South. Tyler and Murphy also discussed Mexico's acquiescence to slavery, even though it did not conform to their own morals of freedom and independence, because of the perceived economic benefits of slave labor.
3. Calvert, *The History of Texas*, 65–66; Federal Writer's Program, "The Negro in Texas."
4. Campbell, *An Empire for Slavery*, 14–32.
5. Federal Writer's Program, *Blacks in Texas*; Tyler and Murphy, *The Slave Narratives of Texas*, xl–xli.

6. Ibid.
7. Campbell, *Gone to Texas*, 221.
8. Federal Writer's Program, *Blacks in Waco*.
9. Calvert, *The History of Texas*, 66; Campbell, *An Empire for Slavery*, 257–258; Mintz, *African American Voices*, 101.
10. Calvert, *The History of Texas*, 65–66; Miliatos, *Some Aspects of Slavery*, 1; Genovese, *Roll, Jordan, Roll*, 12; Williams, *Slavery and Freedom in Delaware*, 88; Like Genovese, Miliatos believed it was the overseer, when there was one present, and not the master, that exercised control over the slaves. Williams found that threats of familial separation were an effective tool in slave control. In Delaware and throughout the upper South, Williams found that masters often threatened to sell their rebellious slaves to owners who would most likely treat them harshly. In the eighteenth century, the most feared states were Georgia and the Carolinas. In the nineteenth century, Alabama, Mississippi, Louisiana, Texas, and Arkansas became locations known for their brutal treatment of slaves.
11. Fry, *Night Riders*, 38. Slave control was a necessary part of plantation culture because most whites lived in fear of slave insurrections.
12. Trexler, *Slavery in Missouri*, 65; Stampp, *The Peculiar Institution*, 171; Douglass, *Narrative of the Life of Frederick Douglass*, 66–67. Stampp plainly states that the state conferred the power to punish on the slave owner, and without this power, slavery could not have existed. As a former slave, Douglass described the abuses of such power when he related the murder of a slave at the hands of an overseer. Even when his actions were questioned by the slave's owner, Douglass commented that the overseer callously replied that the murdered slave had become unmanageable and was setting a "dangerous" example to the others on the plantation.
13. Genovese, *Roll, Jordan, Roll*, 32. Genovese clearly states that Southern law prohibited blacks, free or slave, from testifying against whites in court. This allowed whites to literally murder blacks at will without fear of punishment. Although this statute was introduced during the antebellum period in which slaves, and blacks in general, were not considered socially or biologically equal to whites, Southern attitudes and laws changed little during the one hundred years between the antebellum era and the modern civil rights movement. In the 1950s, Emmitt Till, a black teenager from Chicago, was visiting family in Mississippi when he was taken from his uncle's house in the middle of the night. His mutilated body was found days later. When his uncle was asked in court if he knew who took his nephew that night, he bravely identified the defendants. However, they were summarily acquitted because the jury refused to convict white men based solely on the testimony of a black man.
14. Trexler, *Slavery in Missouri*, 75.
15. Leggett, *Slave Narratives*.
16. Jack and Rosa Maddox, *Slave Narratives*.
17. William Paxton, *Slave Narratives*.

142 **Notes**

18. Clarissa Scales, *Slave Narratives*.
19. Leggett, *Slave Narratives*.
20. Mary Reynolds, *Slave Narratives*.
21. Sarah Allen, *Slave Narratives*.
22. Laura Moore, *Slave Narratives*.
23. Marshall Showers, *Slave Narratives*.
24. Emma Countee Wilson, *Slave Narratives*.
25. Jackson, *Slave Narratives*. Also see Stampp, "Rebels and Sambos," 367–368. Stampp made an impassioned plea that historians should view the slave narratives as "hopelessly inadequate" in examining the nature of slavery. His rationale centered on the fact that because slaves were generally illiterate, there exists the real possibility that what was presented as the slaves' voice was in fact that of those abolitionists who edited the manuscripts. He believed the best evidence available for judging the antebellum slave plantation culture comes from those white observers traveling throughout the south. However, in the *Narrative of the Life of Frederick Douglass, an American Slave* Douglass described an incident that further supports Jackson's assertion that slaves were punished for telling the truth about their treatment and were thus conditioned to lie. He told a story of a field hand that unknowingly encountered his master by the road. The master inquired of the slave the kind of treatment he was receiving and he replied that his master did not treat him well, nor did he receive enough food to eat. Douglass continued by stating how the master immediately informed the overseer of this comment and within a few weeks the slave was sold to a slave trader from Georgia. As a result of this experience, Douglass was adamant that slaves were conditioned to misrepresent their treatment for fear of punitive repercussions.
26. It is also worth noting that many of the comments found throughout the Texas narratives hint that it was not slavery that these aged individuals remembered fondly. Instead it was the times of being cared for by someone else and not having the burden of caring for oneself as an elderly person in the midst of poverty and uncertainty of the 1930s. There were several comments referring to food and hunger, which implied that these elderly people were not adequately able to care for themselves. As slaves they benefited from the paternalism of the master, and if they were productive field hands they were treated accordingly. Therefore, the perceptions offered in the narratives were indicative of the times in which the ex-slaves lived and not the times they were recalling from memory.
27. Douglass, *Narrative of the Life of Frederick Douglass*, 62.

Chapter Three

1. Miliatos, *Some Aspects of Slavery*, 17–18.
2. *Telegraph and Texas Register* (Houston), April 10, 1844, *Newspaper Archives*, Box 4H350, University of Texas, Center for American History.
3. *Texas State Gazette*, October 7, 1854.

4. Hannah Scott, *Slave Narratives*.
5. Ibid.
6. Manuel, *Slave Narratives*.
7. Ibid.
8. Lulu Wilson, *Slave Narratives*.
9. Bennett, Jr., *Before the Mayflower*, 88.
10. Weld, *American Slavery as It Is*, 52–53.
11. Stampp, *The Peculiar Institution*, 145–146; Letter from W. S. Smith to Ashbel Smith, July 7, 1854.
12. Mintz, *African American Voices*, 142.
13. Franklin, *From Slavery to Freedom*, 159.
14. Letter from Benjamin Roper to Ashbel Smith, May 3, 1852.
15. Reynolds, *Slave Narratives*.
16. Letter from John Groesbuck to Ashbel Smith, June 16, 1840.
17. Scott and Andy Anderson, *Slave Narratives*.
18. Campbell Davis, *Slave Narratives*.
19. Agatha Babino, *Slave Narratives*. This narrative illustrates two important aspects of the slave community. The first was the lengths many slave parents went to in protecting their children from abusive punishments. The second involved the decision, and sometimes the futility, in the decision to flee the plantation. Although Babino's aunt's failed in her attempt to escape the plantation, it nonetheless illustrated that many slaves felt they had some options in the control of their own lives. In other words, running away was as viable an option as blind obedience.
20. William Byrd, *Slave Narratives*.
21. Weld, *American Slavery as It Is*, 54.
22. Mother Anne Clark, *Slave Narratives*.
23. Campbell, *An Empire for Slavery*, 144–145.
24. Ben Simpson, *Slave Narratives*.
25. Booker T. Washington expressed the same sentiment in his speech before the Atlanta Exposition in 1895. In what became known as the Atlanta Compromise speech, Washington urged his mostly white audience to reconsider the relationship between Southerners, both white and black. His passionate address centered on the economic benefits to both Southern blacks and whites who joined together for their "mutual benefit," and that they were inexplicably linked because of the nature of slavery.
26. Genovese, *Roll, Jordan, Roll*, 3.
27. Ibid, 5.
28. Bassett, *Slavery in the State of North Carolina*, 82–83.
29. Will Adams, *Slave Narratives*.
30. Eli Coleman, *Slave Narratives*.
31. Weld, *American Slavery as It Is*, 62–63.
32. Davis, *Slave Narratives*.

144 **Notes**

33. Boney, *Slave Life in Georgia*, 59.
34. Van Moore, *Slave Narratives*.
35. Moody, *Slavery on Louisiana Sugar Plantations*, 19.
36. McComb, *Texas*, 60.
37. Franklin, *From Slavery to Freedom*, 146; Hudson, *To Have and to Hold*, 127. Masters also employed professional overseers when they were absentee landowners or simply wanted to maintain some distance from the fields and their slaves. They still made frequent visits to the fields, however but only to converse and provide instruction to the overseers.
38. Franklin, *From Slavery to Freedom*, 147.
39. Moody, *Slavery on Louisiana Sugar Plantations*, 21; Bassett, *The Southern Plantation Overseer*, 3.
40. Liston, *Slavery in America*, 74.
41. Franklin, *From Slavery to Freedom*, 147; Moody, *Slavery on Louisiana Sugar Plantations*, 21; Bassett, *Slavery in the State of North Carolina*, 84–85.
42. Bassett, *The Southern Plantation Overseer*, 3.
43. L. Wilson, *Slave Narratives*.
44. A. Anderson, *Slave Narratives*.
45. L. Wilson, *Slave Narratives*.
46. Trexler, *Slavery in Missouri*, 209; Boles, *Black Southerners*, 83, 112; Moody, *Slavery on Louisiana Sugar Plantations*, 22; Weld, *American Slavery as It Is*, 69.
47. See Adams, Davis, and Green Cumby, *Slave Narratives*.
48. Campbell, *An Empire for Slavery*, 127; Hudson, *To Have and to Hold*, 127; Mintz, *African American Voices*, 111; Also see Cato Carter and Josephine Howard, *Slave Narratives*.
49. Sarah Ford, *Slave Narratives*.

Chapter Four

1. Franklin, *From Slavery to Freedom*, 146. Whites believed blacks were so lazy that they would not be productive without the constant supervision and prodding of whites. Therefore, blacks' perception of slavery and their former masters was closely related to their former work-related interactions with their masters or his agents.
2. Mintz, *African American Voices*, 23; Weld, *American Slavery As It Is*, 35–36; Taylor, *Negro Slavery in Louisiana*, 15; Kolchin, *American Slavery*, 94; Cade, "Out of the Mouths of Ex-Slaves," 308–309; Campbell, *An Empire for Slavery*, 95. Although there were different crops harvested on Southern plantations, the need for cheap labor became *the* motivating factor in the establishment of slavery in this country. In Texas, slave labor was crucial to the state's profitable agricultural economy.
3. Lynch, *Lynch Manifesto*. In 1712, Lynch made his infamous speech to a gathering of slave owners in Virginia. He believed the most efficient way to ensure the plantation operated in a manner to maximize profits was the effective

control of slave labor. He argued that hangings were an inefficient manner of control because of the loss of "stock," but it also led to slave rebellions. He believed the most efficient methods of control were the identification of the physical differences among the slaves and used them to disrupt the cohesiveness of the slave community. Lynch anticipated that such a disruption would lead to the slaves not trusting one another, but instead trusting the slave owner, overseer, or some other white authority. There is currently much debate as to the historical accuracy of this supposed "manifesto." There are some academics that claim this document is an urban myth and appeared magically in the 1990s in the infancy of the Internet. They cite there is no mention of Willie Lynch in any historical document before this time. However, there is no denying the intent of the manifesto in that the control of black slaves were paramount in the minds of slave owners.
4. Richardson, Anderson, Wintz, and Wallace (2001), *Texas*, 186–187; Campbell, *Gone to Texas*, 221. Campbell found that slave owners typically worked their slaves an average of twelve hours per day during the summer months and about ten hours per day during the winter. Most slave owners allowed their slaves to rest on Sundays and half-days on Saturdays. However, this was by no means the golden rule throughout Texas as some worked their slaves seven days a week, especially during the cultivation periods.
5. Mintz, *African American Voices*, 99.
6. Franklin, *From Slavery to Freedom*, 144–145; Stampp, *The Peculiar Institution*, 54.
7. Hudson, *To Have and to Hold*, 2.
8. Adams, *Slave Narratives*.
9. Clara Brim, *Slave Narratives*.
10. Edgar Bendy, *Slave Narratives*.
11. Weld, *American Slavery as It Is*, 94–95.
12. Hudson, *To Have and to Hold*, 2–3, 10–11.
13. Stampp, *The Peculiar Institution*, 54–55.
14. Liston, *Slavery in America*, 74.
15. Boles, *Black Southerners*, 83.
16. Stampp, *The Peculiar Institution*, 54; Campbell, *Gone to Texas*, 221.
17. Austin Grant, *Slave Narratives*.
18. Sarah Ashley, *Slave Narratives*.
19. Genovese, *Roll, Jordan, Roll*, 298. Genovese also found that black slaves developed their own sense of work that was similar to their African ancestors and their agricultural community life. However, he found that it was the demands of slavery and plantation life that ultimately influenced the slaves' attitude toward work and leisure time.
20. A. Anderson, *Slave Narratives*.
21. Paxton, *Slave Narratives*.
22. Ann Hawthorne, *Slave Narratives*.

23. Campbell, *Gone to Texas*, 221; Martin, *More than Chains and Toil*, 10.
24. See the narratives of Holland and Jerry Boykins, *Slave Narratives*; Moody, *Slavery on Louisiana Sugar Plantations*, 45.
25. Moody, *Slavery on Louisiana Sugar Plantations*, 45; Boles, *Black Southerners*, 108.
26. Cade, "Out of the Mouths of Ex-Slaves," 310.
27. Campbell, *Gone to Texas*, 221.
28. Boles, *Black Southerners*, 109. On those large plantations there were a numerous categories of slave responsibilities that included cooks, nursemaids, butlers, and valets, in addition to the field hand.
29. Francis Black, *Slave Narratives*.
30. Fannie Brown, *Slave Narratives*.
31. Kate Darling, *Slave Narratives*.
32. Mary Kincheon Edwards, *Slave Narratives*.
33. Millie Forward, *Slave Narratives*.
34. Boles, *Black Southerners*, 109. Boles also commented on the responsibilities of plantation mammies. Although these women did hold a special place in the plantation household, they seldom wielded an extraordinary influence and power.
35. Joyner, *Down by the Riverside*, 56.
36. William Adams, *Slave Narratives*.
37. Stearlin Arnwine, *Slave Narratives*.
38. Ellen Betts, *Slave Narratives*.
39. Barrett, *Slave Narratives*.
40. Shepard, *Slave Narratives*.
41. Albert Todd, *Slave Narratives*.
42. Emma Watson, *Slave Narratives*.
43. Victor Duhon, *Slave Narratives*.
44. Carter, *Slave Narratives*.
45. Cole, *Slave Narratives*.
46. Campbell, *Gone to Texas*, 221.
47. Brim, *Slave Narratives*.
48. Annie Osborne, *Slave Narratives*.
49. Boles, *Black Southerners*, 111.
50. Joyner, *Down by the Riverside*, 52–54.
51. Harrison Boyd, *Slave Narratives*.
52. Gus Bradshaw, *Slave Narratives*.
53. Mattie Gilmore, *Slave Narratives*.
54. Genovese, *Roll, Jordan, Roll*, 336.

Chapter Five

1. Elkins, *Slavery*, 82. Therefore, this stereotypically racial personality of Sambo was manufactured in the South as a way of defending slavery and the plantation as necessarily paternalistic because blacks were incapable of managing themselves in a civilized society. Even in the slaves' narratives in which the

actions of ex-slaves seemed docile and accommodating, they were often manipulative ruses to obtain certain favors from their owners or overseers.
2. Mary Armstrong, *Slaves Narratives*.
3. Jacob Branch, *Slaves Narratives*.
4. *Matagorda Gazette*, date unknown.
5. *Clarksville Standard*, June 4, 1853.
6. *Clarksville Standard*, June 18, 1853.
7. Williams and Shay, *Time Change*, 34.
8. *Texas Ranger* (Washington County), October 8, 1853.
9. *Texas Gazette* (Austin), March 28, 1854.
10. Coleman, *Slavery Times in Kentucky*, 95–98. Moody, *Slavery on Louisiana Sugar Plantations*, 24–26; Genovese, *Roll, Jordan, Roll*, 617–618; Stampp, *The Peculiar Institution*, 214–215; Hadden, *Slave Patrols*, 47; Mintz, *African American Voices*, 105.
11. Fry, *Night Riders in Black Folk History*, 3.
12. Hadden, *Slave Patrols*, 42.
13. Campbell, *An Empire for Slavery*, 109.
14. Hadden, *Slave Patrols*, 110–113; Also see the narratives of Blanks and Charley Mitchell, *Slave Narratives*.
15. Tom Holland, *Slave Narratives*.
16. Williams, *Slavery and Freedom in Delaware*, 75–78. Williams found some of the slave owners' paranoia was justified. There were many instances in Delaware in which slaves resisted violently to slavery. In one instance a slave refused his master's order to work and threatened him with a knife.
17. Franklin, *From Slavery to Freedom*, 161–162. Franklin described other forms of resistance to include self-mutilation, suicide, and violence toward the slave owners. Franklin also argued that Southern newspapers often carried stories of acts of violence committed by the slave against the slave owner.
18. Proctor, Carter, Blanks, *Slave Narratives*.
19. Richardson, Anderson, Wintz, and Wallace (2001), *Texas*, 187.
20. Campbell, *Gone to Texas*, 226.
21. *Telegraph and Texas Ranger* (Houston), January 15, 1845.
22. *Texas State Gazette*, September 23, 1854.
23. Letter from H. Austin to James Perry, March 5, 1836.
24. Letter from Guy Bryan to J. Perry, September 15, 1851; Handbook of Texas Online, "African Americans."
25. Olmstead, *A Journey Through Texas*, 325. Olmstead also indicated Texas slave owners developed two strategies to prevent slaves from escaping to Mexico. The first involved the placement of armed rangers along the borders. The second comprised the development of a type of insurance fund to be paid by the slave owners and used as rewards when a slave escaped. However, Olmstead's writing failed to indicate which of the two plans, if either, was widely embraced by the beleaguered masters.

26. Haywood, *Slave Narratives*.
27. J. Branch, *Slave Narratives*.
28. William Adams and Harriett Barrett, *Slave Narratives*.
29. Thomas Cole, *Slave Narratives*.
30. Letter from John Cook to P. Rose, March 4, 1849.
31. Memorandum, Julian Devereux, undated.
32. *Texas Ranger*, December 15, 1855.
33. *Texas Gazette* (Austin), February 6, 1830.
34. *Telegraph and Texas Register* (Houston), December 9, 1837.
35. *Texas Republic* (Marshall), September 27, 1851.
36. *Telegraph and Texas Ranger* (Houston), January 1, 1843.
37. *Texas Ranger* (Washington County), March 7, 1850.
38. Letter from G.W. Scott to Thomas Chambers, June 5, 1854.
39. Ibid.
40. *Texas Ranger and Lone Star*, August 25, 1855.
41. Olmstead, *A Journey Through Texas*, 267.
42. Ibid.
43. *Texas Ranger* (Washington County), April 26, 1853.
44. Showers, *Slave Narratives*.
45. Stampp, *The Peculiar Institution*, 617–619.
46. Liston, *Slavery in America*, 196–197.

Chapter Six

1. Kolchin, *American Slavery*, 139–140.
2. Coleman, *Slavery Times in Kentucky*, 57–58; Brown, "Sexuality and the Slave Community," 3, 5.
3. Taylor, *Negro Slavery in Louisiana*, 123; Bennett, Jr., *Before the Mayflower*, 105–107; Moody, *Slavery on Louisiana Sugar Plantations*, 94.
4. Gutman, *The Black Family in Slavery and Freedom*, 70.
5. John Barker, *Slave Narratives*.
6. Phoebe Henderson, *Slave Narratives*.
7. Lucinda Elder, *Slave Narratives* .
8. Ibid.
9. John Ellis, *Slave Narratives*.
10. V. Moore, *Slave Narratives*.
11. Joe Barnes, *Slave Narratives*.
12. Fred Brown, *Slave Narratives*.
13. Betty Powers, *Slave Narratives*.
14. Holland, *Slave Narratives*.
15. Brown, "Sexuality and the Slave Community," 10.
16. McMillen, *Southern Women: Black and White in the Old South*, 13; Herbert Gutman, *The Black Family in Slavery and Freedom*, 52; Also see White, *Ar'n't I a Woman?*

17. William Mathews, *Slave Narratives*.
18. L. Wilson, *Slave Narratives*.
19. Thomas Johns, *Slave Narratives*.
20. Silvia King, *Slave Narratives*.
21. Howard and Sam Jones Washington, *Slave Narratives*.
22. Ford, *Slave Narratives*.
23. Fogel, *Without Consent or Contract*, 455–472.
24. Boles, *Black Southerners*, 69–70.
25. Escott, *Slavery Remembered*, 43–45.
26. Tannenbaum, *Slave and Citizen*, 80–82.
27. Bennett, Jr., *Before the Mayflower*, 105; Douglass, *Narrative of the Life of Frederick Douglass*, 105; Weld, *American Slavery as It Is*, 142.
28. Kolchin, *American Slavery*, 123–124; McMillen, *Southern Women*, 23; Gutman, *The Black Family in Slavery and Freedom*, 396–399. Gutman also found that black men were unable to protect their wives and daughters from the unwanted sexual advances of white males before and after emancipation.
29. Escott, *Slavery Remembered*, 46.
30. Washington, *Invented Lives*, 21–26.
31. McMillen, *Southern Women*, 21–22; Moody, *Slavery on Louisiana Sugar Plantations*, 95; Steven Brown, "Sexuality and the Slave Community," 2–5, 8–10; Taylor, *Negro Slavery in Louisiana*, 19–20, 232.
32. J. and R. Maddox, *Slave Narratives*.
33. Ibid.
34. Reynolds, *Slave Narratives*.
35. Carter, *Slave Narratives*.
36. For a detailed examination of the lives of slave children, see King, *Stolen Childhood*.
37. Stampp, *The Peculiar Institution*, 57–58; Diouf, *Growing up in Slavery*, 44–46. Also see the narratives of Walter Rimm, Jenny Proctor, George Simmons, and John Sneed, *Slave Narratives*.
38. Babino, *Slave Narratives*. Although Babino commented that slave owners often sold their own slave offspring, she also said some masters gave their slave children their freedom.
39. Osborne, *Slave Narratives*.
40. Douglass, *Narrative of the Life of Frederick Douglass*, 49–50.
41. Mother Anne Clark, *Slave Narratives*.
42. Liston, *Slavery in America*, 86–87.
43. McMillen, *Southern Women*, 31–35.
44. Liston, *Slavery in America*, 86–87.
45. Weld, *American Slavery as It Is*, 56.
46. Carter Jackson, *Slave Narratives*.
47. Arnwine, *Slave Narratives*.

48. Howard, *Slave Narratives*. Also see the narratives of Sarah Ashley, Tom Holland, Mary Anderson, Millie Forward, James Jackson, James Hayes, and John Ellis, *Slave Narratives*.
49. Johns and Hagar Lewis, *Slave Narratives*.
50. Barker, *Slave Narratives*.
51. Toby Jones, *Slave Narratives*.
52. Elder, *Slave Narratives*.
53. Boney, *Slave Life in Georgia*, 6.
54. Liston, *Slavery in America*, 93–94.
55. Arnwine, *Slave Narratives*.
56. Louise Mathews, *Slave Narratives*.
57. Annie Row, *Slave Narratives*.
58. Maggie Jackson, *Slave Narratives*.
59. Liston, *Slavery in America*.
60. Fred Brown, *Slave Narratives*.
61. Zek Brown, *Slave Narratives*.
62. See Fry, *Night Riders in Black Folk History*; Gutman, *The Black Family in Slavery and Freedom*, 431.
63. L. Wilson, *Slave Narratives*.
64. Barker, *Slave Narratives*.
65. Bradshaw, *Slave Narratives*.
66. Priscilla Gibson, *Slave Narratives*.
67. Byrd, *Slave Narratives*.
68. James Hayes and Ellen Butler, *Slave Narratives*.
69. Ben Kinchlow, *Slave Narratives*.
70. Rosanna Frazier, *Slave Narratives*.
71. Henderson, *Slave Narratives*.

Chapter Seven

1. A. Anderson, *Slave Narratives*.
2. Taylor, *Negro Slavery in Louisiana*, 109; Kolchin, *American Slavery*, 113; Weld, *American Slavery as It Is*, 34.
3. Kolchin, *American Slavery*, 113; Steckel, "A Peculiar Population," 740.
4. Liston, *Slavery in America*, 78.
5. Stampp, *The Peculiar Institution*, 282–284; Bennett, Jr., *Before the Mayflower*, 89; Mintz, *African American Voices*, 103–104.
6. Holland and Lucy Lewis, *Slave Narratives*; Also see the narrative of Campbell Davis and Toby Jones.
7. Holland, Lorenza Exell, and Mitchell, *Slave Narratives*.
8. Yach Stringfellow, *Slave Narratives*.
9. Sells, *Slave Narratives*.
10. Smalley, *Voices of Slavery*.
11. Liston, *Slavery in America*, 78.

12. Diouf, *Growing up in Slavery*, 36–38.
13. Geneovese, *Roll, Jordan, Roll*, 603–605; Exell, *Slave Narratives*.
14. Powers, *Slave Narratives*.
15. Proctor, *Slave Narratives*.
16. Reynolds, *Slave Narratives*.
17. Richardson, Anderson, Wintz, and Wallace (2001), *Texas*, 186; Campbell, *Gone to Texas*, 223; Coleman, *Slavery Times in Kentucky*, 63–64.
18. Joyner, "The World of the Plantation Slaves," 55–56; Stampp, *The Peculiar Institution*, 290–291; Bennett, Jr., *Before the Mayflower*, 89–90; Boney, *Slave Life in Georgia*, 8. Also see the narratives of Tom Holland, Mary Reynolds, William Matthews, Mary Johnson, Toby Jones, Jenny Proctor, and Ben Kinchlow, *Slave Narratives*.
19. Boney, *Slave Life in Georgia*, 8.
20. Stampp, *The Peculiar Institution*, 289.
21. Weld, *American Slavery as It Is*, 95.
22. Sells, *Slave Narratives*.
23. Arnwine, *Slave Narratives*.
24. Holland, *Slave Narratives*.
25. L. Lewis, *Slave Narratives*.
26. Mintz, *African American Voices*, 107.
27. Campbell, *Gone to Texas*, 223.
28. Mintz, *African American Voices*, 103–104.
29. Bennett, Jr., *Before the Mayflower*, 90.
30. H. Lewis and Reynolds, *Slave Narratives*.
31. Mary Ann Patterson and Cinto Lewis, *Slave Narratives*.
32. J. and R. Maddox, *Slave Narratives*.
33. Ellen Payne, *Slave Narratives*.
34. James W. Smith, *Slave Narratives*.
35. Sneed, *Slave Narratives*.
36. Sells, *Slave Narratives*.
37. Cumby, *Slave Narratives*.
38. Aunt Pinkey Kelly, *Slave Narratives*.
39. Barker, *Slave Narratives*.
40. Taylor, *Negro Slavery in Louisiana*, 129.
41. Anderson and Minerva Edwards, *Slave Narratives*.
42. John Brown, *Slave Narratives*.
43. James Jackson, *Slave Narratives*.
44. Brady, *Slave Narratives*.
45. Charlotte Beverly, *Slave Narratives*.
46. Albert Hill, *Slave Narratives*.
47. Davis, *Slave Narratives*.
48. Will Adams, *Slave Narratives*.
49. Ibid.

50. Charlotte Beverly, *Slave Narratives*.
51. Pauline Johnson, *Slave Narratives*.
52. Payne, *Slave Narratives*.
53. Douglass, *Narrative of the Life of Frederick Douglass*, 135.
54. Hudson, *To Have and to Hold*, 13–20.
55. Moody, *Slavery on Louisiana Sugar Plantations*, 90–91; Kolchin, *American Slavery*, 116.
56. Genovese, *Roll, Jordan, Roll*, 186–193; Martin, *More than Chains and Toil*, 27.
57. Freehling, *The Reintegration of American History*, 71.
58. Kolchin, *American Slavery*, 143–146.
59. William Mathews, *Slave Narratives*.
60. Daniel Phillips, *Slave Narratives*.
61. Cary Davenport, *Slave Narratives*.
62. Martha Patton, *Slave Narratives*.
63. Henry Lewis, *Slave Narratives*. Also see the narrative of James Jackson, *Slave Narratives*.
64. Richard Carruthers, *Slave Narratives*.
65. Wayman Williams, *Slave Narratives*. Also see the narratives of Wes Brady and Wash Anderson, *Slave Narratives*.
66. Butler, *Slave Narratives*.
67. Carruthers, *Slave Narratives*.
68. A. and M. Edwards, *Slave Narratives*.
69. Arnwine, *Slave Narratives*.
70. John Price, *Slave Narratives*.
71. Reynolds, *Slave Narratives*.
72. Willie Ann Smith, *Slave Narratives*.
73. Davis, *Slave Narratives*.
74. Ibid.
75. Byrd, *Slave Narratives*. Also see the narratives of Jenny Proctor and James Boyd, *Slave Narratives*.

Chapter Eight

1. Berlin, Fields, Miller, Reidy, and Rowland, *Free at Last*, 3. Also see Freehling, *The Reintegration of American History*, 114, 139–140; Stampp, *The Era of Reconstruction*, 32–33, 44–45. Freehling argued that Lincoln's support of a constitutional amendment prohibiting federal intervention in the issue of slavery indicated that slavery could not have been the principal cause of the Civil War and that the sixteenth President was ambivalent toward equality for blacks. Stampp found that during the 1850s Lincoln openly confessed that blacks should never be considered equal to whites. Even in the months preceding the Emancipation Proclamation Stampp argued that Lincoln continued having doubts about sudden freedom and favored instead gradual emancipation of Southern blacks.

2. McPherson, *Abraham Lincoln*, vii, 52–53.
3. McPherson, *Battle Cry of Freedom*, 234, 241.
4. Richardson, Anderson, Wintz, and Wallace (2001), *Texas*, 209, 216.
5. Catton, *The Civil War*, 37, 205–206. Catton found that many state leaders complained that Davis was violating civil liberties by forcing individuals to serve an undetermined amount of time in the military. Still, Catton argued, neither Davis nor the new Confederate Congress modified the conscription act.
6. Kelley and Lewis, *To Make Our Own World Anew*, 236.
7. Campbell, *An Empire for Slavery*, 231, 233.
8. See the narratives of Thomas Johns, Harrison Boyd, Lizzie Jones, Elsie Reece, and James Hayes, *Slave Narratives*. Jones said her master came home early from military service because of an illness, whereas Reece, interviewed in Fort Worth, said her slave owner's son come back after having his leg "shot off," and died shortly thereafter because of his injuries. Hayes said his master's body was shipped home and recalled, "All de old folks, cullud and white, was cryin.' Missy Elline she fainted. When de body comes home, dere's a powerful big funeral and after dat, dere's powerful weepin's and sadness on dat place."
9. Ross, *Slave Narratives*.
10. Payne, *Slave Narratives*.
11. Harrison Beckett, *Slave Narratives*. Also see the Narratives of Mary Kindred and Abram Sells, *Slave Narratives*.
12. Willie Forward, *Slave Narratives*. Also see Charley Mitchell, Allen Price, and Harriet Barrett, *Slave Narratives*.
13. Martin Jackson, *Slave Narratives*. Also see Allen Price, whose father, like Jackson's, cautioned him that the end of the war and slavery may not necessary mean improved black-white relationships.
14. William Adams, *Slave Narratives*.
15. A. Anderson, *Slave Narratives*.
16. Jack Bess, *Slave Narratives*.
17. Sells, *Slave Narratives*.
18. Henry Lewis, *Slave Narratives*.
19. James Hayes, *Slave Narratives*.
20. Litwack, *Been in the Storm So Long*, 167–172, 293.
21. Barr, "Change and Continuity in Texas," 97; Freehling, *The Reintegration of American History*, 114, 139–140; Stampp, *The Era of Reconstruction*, 32–33, 44–45.
22. Perman, *Emancipation and Reconstruction*, 11–12.
23. See McPherson's *The Negro's Civil War*, Rose's *Rehearsal for Reconstruction*, and Bentley's *A History of the Freedmen's Bureau*.
24. Campbell, *Gone to Texas*, 268.
25. Stampp, *The Era of Reconstruction*, 59.

26. DuBois, *Black Reconstruction*, 223; Stampp, *The Era of Reconstruction*, 112, 156; Perman, *Emancipation and Reconstruction*, 20; DuBois argued that white Southerners became fearful of and fought the Freedmen's Bureau and the new Radical governments to prevent federal interference with Southern labor and keep the carpetbaggers from placing the former slaves socially and economically ahead of the defeated white South. Stampp argued that Southerners found an ally in President Andrew Johnson who attempted to veto the extension of the Freedmen's Bureau. Johnson believed the Freedmen's Bureau legislation provided blacks with safeguards not even offered to whites. This gives validity to the Southerners' fear that Northern Radicals were trying to upset what they considered the natural social order in which blacks were subservient to whites. Congress nonetheless passed the Freedmen's Bureau legislation over the veto of the president. Perman found the introduction of the new Black Codes resulted from the efforts to preserve the old-racial etiquette that allowed whites to mete out punishment for actions they considered inappropriate.
27. Cox, "General O.O. Howard and the 'Misrepresented Bureau,'" 109.
28. Dubois, *Black Reconstruction* 225.
39. Perman, *Emancipation and Reconstruction*, 36; Bentley, *A History of the Freedmen's Bureau*, 89–102. Although it was true that the Radicals and the leadership in the Freedmen's Bureau believed land in the hands of blacks would ultimately provide them economic independence from their former masters, the land would have to come from the pool of confiscated or abandoned lands obtained after the war. However, the federal government never promised blacks forty acres of land. During the final months of the war General William T. Sherman reserved land along the Georgia and South Carolina coasts for blacks as a way to relieve the burden placed on his army as they drove through the heart of the South destroying everything in their path. Blacks did occupy large tracts of abandoned land, but Johnson returned these lands to the planter aristocracy as part of his Amnesty Plan. Therefore, blacks were left to the economic mercies of bitter whites that wanted to take advantage of their economic vulnerability.
30. Canovan, *Populism*, 100–105. This alliance of black and white farmers coalesced into the Populist Party but proved only occasionally successful. For the most part, however, economic suffering exacerbated old hatreds more than it helped people overcome those antipathies. Furthermore, when Southern white Populist politicians felt cornered, they fell back to familiar racial attitudes of racism and hatred towards blacks.
31. Crouch, *The Freedmen's Bureau*, 12; Smallwood, *Time of Hope, Time of Despair*, 25–26.
32. Alan Price, *Slave Narratives*.
33. Tannenbaum, *Slave and Citizen*, 110–111; Litwack, *Been in the Storm So Long*, 297.
34. Dixon, *East of the River*, 24, 108; Federal Writer's Program, "The Negro in Texas." As news spread about the collapse of slavery, hundreds of freed slaves

left their plantations heading for the nearest city where they believed Union officials would provide food and work. For example, former slaves poured into Houston from Peach Point and other plantations in Brazoria, Fort Bend, and neighboring counties trying to escape oppressiveness and hoping to find displaced family members. In describing the present importance of Juneteenth in her family, Dixon said, "Juneteenth wasn't just any holiday. Next to Christmas, it was the most important holiday of the year."

35. William Adams, *Slave Narratives*.
36. Armstead Barrett, *Slave Narratives*.
37. Martin Ruffin, *Slave Narratives*.
38. Carter, *Slave Narratives*.
39. Phillips, *Slave Narratives*.
40. Tannenbaum, *Slave and Citizen*, 110–111.
41. W. Mathews, *Slave Narratives*.
42. Susan Merrit, *Slave Narratives*.
43. William Thomas, *Slave Narratives*.
44. Julia Malone, *Slave Narratives* . Malone also described her owner was a powerful man before slaves were freed and "acts like de cock of de walk. All dat changes after freedom. I seed him layin' in the sun like de dog. I offers to wash he clothes and he jus' grunt. He done turned stone deaf, and de white folks say it 'cause he done treat he slaves so bad."
45. Rimm, *Slave Narratives*.
46. Row, *Slave Narratives*.
47. *Ibid.* Also see Lu Perkins, *Slave Narratives*. Perkins recalled how her former owner was devastated "on account of losing his darkeys" and told his slaves, "You is free on account of the war. You don't have to stay no place where you don't want to stay, but if you want to stay here you can." Even though he was unsure of his own future, Perkins' former owner gave her father two hundred acres of land. However, Perkins commented to her interviewer that her former owner's sons prevented her father from assuming possession of the land.
48. Jack Bess, *Slave Narratives*.
49. Peter Mitchell, *Slave Narratives*.
50. Holland, *Slave Narratives*.
51. Will Adams, *Slave Narratives*.
52. C. Mitchell, *Slave Narratives*.
53. Johns, *Slave Narratives*.
54. Litwack, *Been in the Storm So Long*, 340–341.
55. Liza Jones, *Slave Narratives*.
56. Watson, *Slave Narratives*.
57. Paxton, *Slave Narratives*.
58. Alica Houston, *Slave Narratives*.
59. Litwack, *Been in the Storm So Long*, 331.
60. Kelly, *Slave Narratives*.

61. Powers, *Slave Narratives*.
62. Lewis Jones, *Slave Narratives*.
63. Litwack, *Been in the Storm So Long*, 343.
64. Lu Perkins, *Slave Narratives*.
65. Lu Lee, *Slave Narratives*.
66. Rimm, *Slave Narratives*.
67. A. Anderson, *Slave Narratives*.
68. Ross, *Slave Narratives*.

Chapter Nine

1. The narrative of Andrew Goodman describes how the son of the former master cheated Goodman's father out of money after agreeing to a sharecropping contract.
2. The following served the Freedmen's Bureau in Texas as assistant commissioners: Edgar M. Gregory (September 1865–May 1866), Joseph Kiddoo (May 1866–January 1867), Charles Griffin (January 1867–September 1867), Joseph J. Reynolds (September 1867–January 1869), Edward R. S. Canby (November 1868–March 1869) and Joseph Reynolds (January 1869–July 1870). William Richter and Barry Crouch examined the roles of the Freedmen's Bureau in Texas in *Overreached on All Sides: The Freedmen's Bureau Administrators in Texas, 1865–1868*, and *The Freedmen's Bureau and Black Texans*, respectively. Richter's findings indicate that the bureaucratic nature of the Freedmen's Bureau kept it from making real significant contributions to Texas' postwar society. He also found that those Texans that remained loyal to the Confederate cause routinely terrorized blacks, bureau agents, and Union army soldiers. Crouch's argument followed along the same lines, but he chose to focus on the bureau's activities in a single district in east Texas. Like Crouch and Richter, Randy Finley studied the Freedmen's bureau in Arkansas following the case study approach. In *From Slavery to Uncertain Freedom: The Freedmen's Bureau in Arkansas*, Finely examined the bureau from the perspective of blacks and poor whites. He found that many of the policies of the bureau in Arkansas were racially motivated, but the agency still contributed to the transition of blacks from slaves to freemen. In Louisiana, Howard White found similar conditions as those in Texas and Arkansas. But what makes *The Freedmen's Bureau in Louisiana* valuable in the local study of the bureau is the relationship between blacks who were already transitioning into freedmen before the end of the Civil War and the Freedmen's Bureau with its traditional problems of racism and corruption. Blacks were already moving onto land abandoned by white planters before the bureau official began operations in the state. Not only were blacks moving to abandoned lands, but they were also flocking to the cities, such as New Orleans, trying the escape the remnants of rural slavery.
3. Ronald Butchart and Robert Morris presented studies that emphasized the role of education to the Freedmen's Bureau's Southern agenda. However, they disagreed

to the extent that the objectives of educating blacks were not consistent with their public rhetoric. In *Northern Schools, Southern Blacks and Reconstruction*, Butchart argued that educating blacks was a means of exercising social control. On the other hand, Morris, in *Reading, 'Riting, and Reconstruction*, focused on the in-fighting between the missionaries on the manner in which blacks were to be educated.
4. Rosina Hoard, *Slave Narratives*.
5. Bureau of Refugees, *Freedmen and Abandoned Lands, 1865–1869*, James Johnson. In his narrative, James Johnson recalled how local whites disapproved of the formal education the Freedmen's Bureau provided the former slaves and how the white northern teachers were often criticized for helping blacks.
6. Wayman Williams, *Slave Narratives*.
7. Bureau of Refugees M821, roll 32, Bureau of Refugees, Miscellaneous Records Relating to Murders and other Criminal Offenses Committed in Texas 1865–1868. The Houston area included Harris, Liberty, Brazoria, Montgomery, and Fort Bend Counties. The classification "assault" included all acts involving whipping, shooting, stabbing, or beatings.
8. Bureau of Refugees, Miscellaneous Records Relating to Murders; Letter from ME Davis to HA Ellis, October 13, 1866, Bureau of Refugees, M821, roll 32.
9. Lu Perkins, *Slave Narratives*.
10. Bud Jones, *Slave Narratives*.
11. The thesis that blacks were mere pawns to the North's desire to punish the South was explored in Smallwood's *Time of Hope, Time of Despair*. He found that blacks had limited political power during the Reconstruction, and the power did they exercise was only at the consent of the minority white Republicans.
12. Letter from L. Shoemaker to EM Pease, June 23, 1868, Bureau of Refugees, M821, roll 32.
13. Ibid.
14. Perman, *Emancipation and Reconstruction*, 94–95. Perman argued that the initial objective of the Klan was the redemption of the South from the imposed Radical, or "Negro," governments. Put of this redemption involved the intimidation of voters, black and white. "Although attempts by local whites to control blacks socially and economically may also have been involved, the Klan's overall aim was almost certainly political."
15. Stampp, *The Era of Reconstruction*, 199–201; Franklin, *From Slavery to Freedom*, 275.
16. Will Adams, *Slave Narratives*.
17. Campbell, *Gone to Texas*, 281; Richardson, et al., *Texas*, 244.
18. William Hamilton, *Slave Narratives*.
19. Ibid.
20. Perkins, *Slave Narratives*.
21. Lee, *Slave Narratives*.
22. James Martin, *Slave Narratives*.

23. B. Jones, *Slave Narratives*.
24. J. and R. Maddox, *Slave Narratives*.
25. Ibid.
26. Ibid.
27. Barr, *Black Texans*, 153–154. The number of black farm owners continued at about 20,000 in 1940, however black tenants declined in the 1930s from 65,00 to 32,000.
28. Richardson, Anderson et al., *Texas,* 384 ; Patenaude, *Texans, Politics, and the New Deal*, 87–91, 100; Kingston, *A Concise of History of Texas*, 201; Haley, *From Spindletop through World War II*, 183–184. Texas's political leaders originally supported Roosevelt and the New Deal. However, by the end of the 1930s, political support for the New Deal was waning, much as it was throughout the country. Governor Miriam "Ma" Ferguson created the Texas Relief Commission with federal funds to coordinate relief efforts between private and public agencies. However, Ma Ferguson and her husband, former governor Jim Ferguson, were soon accused of using relief funds to create a patronage machine to reward supporters and punish opponents. Eventually, the Texas Relief Commission and the Ferguson administration came under scrutiny when allegations of fiscal mismanagement of federal funds were made. Regardless of fiscal irregularities, the first federal grant of $808,429 arrived on June 27, 1933, and by the end of Roosevelt's first term approximately $1.5 billion were "pumped into the state's economy." When James Allred, former state attorney general and avowed New Dealer, became Texas's governor in 1935, he spent his first term "tidying up after the Fergusons—revamping the Texas Rangers from hundreds of Ma's 'special' commissions, and creating an independent board to govern pardons and paroles from the prison system." Three years later, W. Lee O'Daniel replaced Allred as governor and continued his predecessor's policy of seeking increased federal funding for work relief. However, Roosevelt's court packing scheme damaged his, and the New Deal's, reputation in Texas. O'Daniel remarked, "I am not saying that all of Mr. Roosevelt's plans are sound and right, but as long as he has the national grab bag open and as long as other states are grabbing, I'm gonna grab all I can for the State of Texas."
29. Stimpson, Jr., *A Black Sharecropper's Recollections*, 19.
30. *The Houston-Post Dispatch*, November 4, 1930.
31. Richardson, *Texas*, 384.
32. Letter from Lonita Gourley to Franklin Roosevelt.
33. Hill, *Dallas*, 129–130.
34. Johnson, *Houston*, 285. Even though racism existed in Houston, the author made sure the reader understood that benevolent organizations (churches) provided relief to all Houstonians regardless of "race and creed."
35. Kingston, *A Concise of History of Texas*, 200.
36. Patenaude, *Texans, Politics, and the New Deal*, 107. In his article, "The Civilian Conservation Corps and the Negro," John Salmond also found that racism in

the management of CCC camps was not restricted to Texas. Throughout the South blacks were systematically excluded from selection to CCC facilities, even though in many counties blacks constituted more than 50 percent of the population. Salmond also found the issue of racism in the selection process reached Roosevelt who failed to challenge the South's continued segregation and degradation of blacks. As with the issue of lynching, the president decided he would not risk his larger New Deal programs or his reputation by coming to the aid of blacks.
37. Richardson, *Texas*, 384.
38. Two studies by Arnoldo De León illustrated the history and racism experienced by the Hispanic community in Texas. In *They Called Them Greasers*, De León focused on the discrimination faced by Mexicans during the period 1821–1900. He found that whites in Texas believed Mexicans were culturally inferior, Mexican women to be sexually promiscuous, and overall they could not be trusted to be loyal American citizens. Like blacks, Mexicans were routinely murdered and lynched. In *Ethnicity in the Sunbelt*, De León focused on the building of Mexican communities in Houston. In the 1930s he found the Mexican community used the same strategy for survival as the black community, reliance on churches, cultural maintenance, and community self-reliance. Even though many Mexicans returned to Mexico during the depression, De León found that those who stayed in Houston tried to end systematic racism through civil rights organizations: Latin American Club, League of United Latin American Citizens, and in the 1960s, La Raza. Likewise, in *The World of the Mexican Worker in Texas*, Emilio Zamora found those Mexican communities along Texas' border regions, like those in the urban areas, also established social and labor organizations as a way of confronting the hardships of the depression.
39. Holden, "After-School Careers of Negro High School Graduates," 48–54.
40. *Houston Chronicle*, August 4, 1996; *The Informer* (Houston), March 9, 1940, March 16, 1940, January 8, 1949, January 21, 1956, April 21, 1956, April 28, 1956, June 18, 1956, August 4, 1996.
41. *San Antonio Light*, October 20, 1940.
42. Ibid.
43. Ibid.
44. The building used for this segregated school was only 30' X 35', and local blacks purchased the tin roof for only ten dollars.
45. WPA, Narrative Report, District 4, September 1940.
46. WPA, Narrative Report, District 1, November 1940.
47. Ibid.
48. Ibid.
49. WPA, Narrative Report, District 16, March 1940.
50. Letter from Dorothy Wentland to Virginia Chapman, November 23, 1940, WPA, WPA Narrative Report, District 1, December 1940.
51. Ibid.

160 Notes

52. WPA, Narrative Report, District 10, May 1940.
53. WPA, Statewide Narrative Report, October 1940.
54. WPA, Narrative Records, District 10, 1940.
55. WPA, Statewide Narrative Report, October 1940.
56. Ibid.; WPA, Narrative Report, District 1, November 1940; WPA, Narrative Report, District 6, November 1940; WPA, Narrative Report, District 10, November 1940.
57. WPA, Narrative Report, District 4, December 1940.
58. Ibid.
59. WPA, Narrative Report, District 10, May 1940.
60. Letter of resignation from James Valentine, Narrative Report, District 10, November 1940.
61. Aleck Trimble, *Slave Narratives*.
62. Aaron Russell, *Slave Narratives*. Also see the narrative of Willis Winn who said he was surviving the depression through the generosity of local whites. He said, "If it wasn't for good white folks, I'd starve to death."
63. Diane Watson, *Slave Narratives*.
64. Willis Winn, *Slave Narratives*.
65. John McCoy, *Slave Narratives*.
66. Bert Strong, *Slave Narratives*.
67. Rose Williams, *Slave Narratives*.
68. Louis Love, *Slave Narratives*.

Chapter Ten

1. There is a vast amount of literature on the Roosevelt administration and New Deal programs and includes: Schlesinger, Jr., *The Age of Roosevelt*; McElvaine, *The Great Depression*; Howard, *The WPA and Federal Relief Policy*; Larson, "The Cultural Projects of the WPA".
2. Rhodes, *History of the United States*.
3. Hart, *Slavery and Abolition*.
4. Elkins, *Slavery*, 8.
5. Phillips, *American Negro Slavery*. Also see Franklin, *From Slavery to Freedom*, 148.
6. Elkins, *Slavery*, 13.
7. Hofstadter, "U.B. Phillips and the Plantation Legend," 109–124; Stampp, "The Historian and the Southern Negro Slavery," 614.
8. Aptheker, *American Negro Slavery*.
9. Elkins, *Slavery*, 82.
10. Campbell, *An Empire for Slavery*, 6.
11. See Stampp, *The Peculiar Institution*.
12. Stampp, "The Historian and Southern Negro Slavery," 616.
13. By the 1950s most scholars rejected Phillips' racist opinion that blacks were biologically inferior to whites. What was at issue now was to what degree did

black slaves create and maintain their culture, familial relations, and their lives immediately after emancipation despite the oppressive nature of slavery and the plantation community.
14. Cade, "Out of the Mouths of Ex-Slaves," 294–337.
15. Ibid, 294.
16. Yetman. "Background of the Slave Narrative Collection," 534–553; Rawick. *The American Slave*.
17. Blassingame, *The Slave Community*.
18. Escott, *Slavery Remembered*.
19. Gutman, *The Black Family in Slavery and Freedom*.
20. Fry, *Night Rider's in Black Folk History*.
21. Joyner, *Down by the Riverside*.
22. White, *Ar'n't I A Woman?*.
23. Litwack, *Been in the Storm So Long*.
24. See Shaw, "Using the WPA Ex-Slave Narratives,"623–658.
25. Ron Tyler and Lawrence R. Murphy, *The Slave Narratives of Texas* (Austin: Encino Press, 1974).
26. Campbell, *An Empire for Slavery*.
27. Smallwood, *Time of Hope, Time of Despair*; Pitre, "A Note on the Historiography of Blacks," 340–348.
28. Weiss, *Farewell to the Party of Lincoln*.
29. Sitkoff, *A New Deal for Blacks*; Kusmer, *A Ghetto Takes Shape*; Osofsky, *Harlem*; Drake, *Black Metropolis*; Spear, *Black Chicago*; and Borchet, *Alley Life in Washington D.C.*.
30. Barr, *Black Texans*; Hine, *Black Victory*; Pitre, *In Struggle Against Jim Crow*; and Beeth and Wintz, *Black Dixie*.

I will bless the LORD at all times;
His praise shall continually be in my mouth.
My soul will make its boast in the LORD;
The humble will hear it and rejoice.
O magnify the LORD with me, and let us exalt
His name together.
Psalms 34:1-3

BIBLIOGRAPHY

Primary Sources

Stephen F. Austin Papers, Center for American History, University of Texas.
Bureau of Refugees, Freedmen and Abandoned Lands, 1865–1869, National Archives M821, roll 32, University of Houston, Archives
Bureau of Refugees, Freedmen and Abandoned Lands, 1865–1869, Miscellaneous Records Relating to Murders and other Criminal Offenses Committed in Texas 1865–1868, University of Houston Archives
Thomas Chambers Papers, Center for American History, University of Texas.
Clarksville Standard, June 4, 1853, Box 4H350, *WPA Records*, Center for American History, University of Texas.
Julian Devereux Papers, Center for American History, University of Texas.
Federal Writer's Program, "The Negro in Texas," Box 4H350, Center for American History, University of Texas.
Federal Writer's Program, *Blacks in Texas*, WPA Fact Book, Center for American History, University of Texas.
Federal Writer's Program, *Blacks in Waco*, Box, 4J252, Center for American History, University of Texas.
Houston-Post Dispatch, November 4, 1930, Center for American History, University of Texas.
Matagorda Gazette, date unknown, Box 4H350, *WPA Records*, Center for American History, University of Texas.
Narrative Report, District 4, September 1940, Center for American History, University of Texas.
James and Stephen Perry Papers, Center for American History, University of Texas.
Preston Rose Papers, Center for American History, University of Texas.
Slave Narratives, Box 4H359, Center for American History, University of Texas.
Ashbel Smith Papers, Center for American History, University of Texas.
Telegraph and Texas Register (Houston), April 10, 1844, *Newspaper Archives*, Box4H350, Center for American History, University of Texas.
Telegraph and Texas Ranger (Houston), January 15, 1845, Box 4H350, *WPA Records*, Center for American History, University of Texas.
Texas Gazette (Austin), March 28, 1854, Box 4H350, *WPA Records*, Center for American History, University of Texas.
Texas Ranger (Washington County), October 8, 1853, Box 4H350, *WPA Records*, Center for American History, University of Texas.

Texas Ranger and Lone Star, August 25, 1855, Center for American History, University of Texas.

Texas Republic (Marshall), September 27, 1851, Box 4H350, Center for American History, University of Texas.

Texas State Gazette, September 23, 1854, Box 4H350, *WPA Records*, Center for American History, University of Texas.

Secondary Sources

Aptheker, Herbert. *American Negro Slavery*. New York: International Publishers, 1943.

Barr, Alwyn. *Black Texans: A History of African Americans in Texas, 1528–1995* Norman: University of Oklahoma Press, 1996.

Barr, Alwyn. "Change and Continuity in Texas during the Civil War and Reconstruction." In *Texas Heritage*, edited by Ben Procter and Archie P. McDonald, pp. 97–112. Arlington Heights, IL: Harlan Davidson, 1992.

Bassett, John Spencer. *Slavery in the State of North Carolina*. Baltimore: Johns Hopkins Press, 1899.

———. *The Southern Plantation Overseer*. Westport, Conn.: Negro University Press, 1925.

Bennett, Jr., Lerone. *Before the Mayflower: A History of Black America*. 6th ed. New York: Penguin Books, 1988.

Bentley, George. *A History of the Freedmen's Bureau*. New York: Octagon Books, 1974.

Beeth, Howard, and Cary Wintz, *Black Dixie*. College Station: Texas A&M University Press, 1992.

Berlin, Ira, Barbara J. Fields, Steven F. Miller, Joseph P. Reidy, and Leslie S. Rowland, eds. *Free at Last*. New York: The New Press, 1992.

Billington, Ray Allen. "Government and the Arts: The W.P.A. Experience." *American Quarterly*, 4 (Winter 1961): 466–479.

Blassingame, John. *The Slave Community*. New York: Oxford University Press, 1972.

Blassingame, John. "Using the Testimony of Ex-Slave: Approaches and Problems." *The Journal of Southern History*, 4 (November 1975): 473–492.

Boles, John. *Black Southerners, 1619–1869*. Lexington: University of Kentucky Press, 1983.

Boney, F. N. *Slave Life in Georgia: A Narrative of the Life, Sufferings, and the Escape of John Brown: A Fugitive Slave*. Savannah: A Beehive Press Book, 1991.

Borchet, James. *Alley Life in Washington D.C.* Urbana: University of Illinois Press, 1980.

Botkin, Benjamin A. *Lay My Burden Down: A Folk History of Slavery*. Chicago: University of Chicago Press, 1945.

Brown, Steven. "Sexuality and the Slave Community." *Phylon*, 42 (1981), 1–10.

Cade, John B. "Out of the Mouths of Ex-Slaves." *The Journal of Negro History* 20, (July 1935): 294–337.

Calvert, Robert. *The History of Texas*. Wheeling, IL: Harlan Davidson, 1996.

Campbell, Randolph. *An Empire for Slavery: The Peculiar Institution in Texas, 1821–1865*. Baton Rouge: Louisiana State University Press, 1989.

Campbell, Randolph. *Gone to Texas*. New York: Oxford University Press, 2003.
Catton, Bruce. *The Civil War*. Boston: Houghton Mifflin Company, 1987.
Canovan, Margaret. *Populism*. New York: Harcourt Brace Jovanovich, 1981.
Coleman, Winston I. *Slavery Times in Kentucky*. Chapel Hill: University of North Carolina Press, 1940.
Cox, John, and Lawanda Cox. "General O.O. Howard and the 'Misrepresented Bureau.'" *Journal of Southern History* 19 (1953): 428–429.
Crouch, Barry. *The Freedmen's Bureau and Black Texas*. Austin: University of Texas Press, 1992.
de León, Arnold. *Ethnicity in the Sunbelt*. College Station: Texas A&M University Press, 2001.
de León, Arnold. *They Called Them Greasers*. Austin: University of Texas Press, 1983.
Dixon, Addie Mae Barret. *East of the River*. Houston: Barrett Historical Society, 1999.
Diouf, Sylviane. *Growing up in Slavery*. Brookfield, Conn.: The Millbrook Press, 2001.
Douglass, Frederick. *Narrative of the Life of Frederick Douglass, an American Slave*. New York: Penguin Books, 1982.
Drake, St. Clair. *Black Metropolis*. New York: Harper Row, 1962.
DuBois, W. E. B. *Black Reconstruction*. New York: Russell & Russell, 1935.
Fisk University Social Science Institute. *Unwritten History of Slavery: Autobiographical Accounts of Negro Ex-Slaves*. Washington: Microcard Editions, 1968.
Elkins, Stanley. *Slavery: A Problem in American Institutional and Intellectual Life*. Chicago: University of Chicago Press, 1968.
Escott, Paul. *Slavery Remembered*. Chapel Hill: University of North Carolina Press, 1979.
Fisk University Social Science Institute. *God Struck Me Dead: Religion Conversion Experiences and Autobiographies of Ex-Slaves*. Nashville, 1945.
Fogel, Robert William. *Without Consent or Contract*. New York: W. W. Norton and Company, 1992.
Franklin, John Hope. *From Slavery to Freedom: A History of African Americans*. Boston: McGraw-Hill, 2000.
Freehling, William. *The Reintegration of American History: Slavery and the Civil War*. New York: Oxford University Press, 1994.
Fry, Gladys-Marie. *Night Rider's in Black Folk History*. Knoxville: University of Tennessee Press, 1984.
Genovese, Eugene. *Roll, Jordan, Roll: The World the Slaves Made*. New York: Pantheon, 1974.
Gorn, Elliott J. "Black Spirits: The Ghostlore of Afro American Slaves." *American Quarterly* 36 (1984): 549–565.
Gutman, Herbert. *The Black Family in Slavery and Freedom*. New York: Pantheon Books, 1976.
Hadden, Sally E. *Slave Patrols: Law and Violence in Virginia and the Carolinas*. Cambridge: Harvard University Press, 2001.

Haley, James. *From Spindletop through World War II*. New York: St. Martin's Press, 1993.
Handbook of Texas Online. "African Americans." Available at http://www.tshaonline.org/handbook/online/articles/pkaan, accessed August 29, 2013.
Hart, Albert Bushnell. *Slavery and Abolition, 1831–1841*. New York: Harper, 1906.
Hill, Patricia Everage. *Dallas: The Making of a Modern City*. Austin: University of Texas Press, 1996.
Hine, Darlene Clark. *Black Victory: The Rise and fall of the White Primary in Texas*. Millwood, NY: KTO Press, 1979.
Hofstadter, Richard. "U. B. Phillips and the Plantation Legend." *Journal of Negro History* xxix (April 1944): 109–124.
Holden, P. H. "After-School Careers of Negro High School Graduates of Houston, Texas, 1933." *The Journal of Negro Education* 7, no. 1 (January 1938): 48–54.
Howard, Donald S. *The WPA and Federal Relief Policy*. New York: Russell Sage Foundation, 1943.
Hudson, Larry. *To Have and to Hold: Slave Work and Family Life in Antebellum South Carolina*. Athens: University of Georgia Press, 1997.
Johnson, Marguerite. *Houston: The Unknown City 1836–1946*. College Station: Texas A&M University Press, 1991.
Joyner, Charles. *Down by the Riverside: A South Carolina Slave Community*. Urbana: University of Illinois Press, 1984.
Kelley, Robin D. G., and Earl Lewis. *To Make Our Own World Anew*. Oxford: Oxford University Press, 2000.
King, Wilma. *Stolen Childhood*. Bloomington: Indiana University Press, 1995.
Kingston, Mike. *A Concise of History of Texas*. Houston: Gulf Publishing Company, 1991.
Kolchin, Peter. *American Slavery, 1619–1877*. New York: Hill and Wang, 1993.
Kusmer, Kenneth. *A Ghetto Takes Shape: Black Cleveland, 1870–1930*. Urbana: University of Illinois Press, 1976.
Larson, Cedric. "The Cultural Projects of the WPA." *The Public Opinion Quarterly* 3 (July 1939): 491–496.
Liston, Robert. *Slavery in America*. New York: McGraw-Hill, 1970.
Litwack, Leon. *Been in the Storm So Long*. New York: Knopf, 1979.
Lynch, Willie. "Lynch Manifesto." Available at thetalkingdrum.com/wil.html, accessed on August 29, 2013.
Mangione, Jerre. *The Dream and the Deal: The Federal Writers' Project, 1935–1943*. Philadelphia: University of Pennsylvania Press, 1983.
Martin, Joan. *More than Chains and Toil: A Christian Work Ethic of Enslaved Women*. Louisville: Westminster John Knox Press, 2000.
McComb, David G. *Texas: A Modern History*. Austin: University of Texas Press, 1989.
McElvaine, Robert. *The Great Depression: America, 1929–1941*. New York: Times Books, 1993.
McMillen, Sally. *Southern Women: Black and White in the Old South*. Arlington Heights, Ill.: Harlan Davidson, 2002.

McPherson, James. *Abraham Lincoln and the Second American Revolution*. Oxford: Oxford University Press, 1991.
McPherson, James. *Battle Cry of Freedom*. Oxford University Press, 2003.
Mintz, Steven. *African American Voices*. 3rd ed. St. James, N.Y.: Brandywine Press, 2004.
Olmstead, Frederick Law. *A Journey through Texas*. New York: Dix, Edwards and Co., 1857.
Osofsky, Gilbert. *Harlem: The Making of a Ghetto*. New York: Harper Row, 1966.
Patenaude, Lionel. *Texans, Politics, and the New Deal*. New York: Garland, 1983.
Perman, Michael. *Emancipation and Reconstruction, 1862–1879*. Wheeling, IL: Harlan Davidson, Inc, 1987.
Phillips, Ulrich B., *American Negro Slavery: A Survey of the Supply, Employment and Control of Negro Labor as Determined by the Plantation Regime*. New York: Appleton, 1918.
Pitre, Merlene. "A Note on the Historiography of Blacks in the Reconstruction of Texas." *The Journal of Negro History* 66 (Winter 1981): 340–348.
Pitre, Merline. *In Struggle Against Jim Crow: Lulu B. White and the NAACP, 1900–1957*. College Station: Texas A&M University Press, 1999.
Rawick, George. *The American Slave: A Composite Autobiography*. Westport, Conn.: Greenwood Publishing Co., 1972.
Rhodes, James Ford. *History of the United States from the Compromise of 1850 to the Final Restoration of Home Rule in the South in 1877*. New York: MacMillan, 1893.
Richardson, Rupert, Adrian Anderson, Cary Wintz, Ernest Wallace. *Texas: The Lone Star State*, 8th ed. Upper Saddle River, NJ: Prentice Hall, 2001.
Rose, Nancy *Put to Work: Relief Programs in the Great Depression*. New York: Monthly Review Press, 1993.
Salmond, John. "The Civilian Conservation Corp and the Negro," *The Journal of American History* 52 (June 1965): 75–88.
Shaw, Stephanie. "Using the WPA Ex-Slave Narratives to Study the Impact of the Great Depression." *The Journal of Southern History* LXIX (August 2003): 623–658.
Sitkoff, Harvard. *A New Deal for Blacks: The Emergence of Civil Rights as a National Issue*. New York: Oxford University Press, 1978.
Smallwood, James. *Time of Hope, Time of Despair: Black Texans during Reconstruction*. New York: Kennikat Press, 1981.
Spear, Allan. *Black Chicago: The Making of a Negro Ghetto, 1890–1920*. Chicago: University of Chicago Press, 1967.
Stampp, Kenneth. "Rebels and Sambos: The Search for the Negro's Personality in Slavery." *The Journal of Southern History* 3 (August 1971): 367–392.
Stampp, Kenneth. *The Era of Reconstruction, 1865–1877*. New York: Vintage Books, 1967.
Stampp, Kenneth. "The Historian and Southern Negro Slavery." *The Journal of American Historical Review* 57 (April 1952): 613–624.

Stampp, Kenneth. *The Peculiar Institution: Slavery in the Ante-Bellum South*. New York: Alfred Knopf, 1956.

Steckel, Richard . "A Peculiar Population: The Nutrition, Health, and Mortality of American Slaves from Childhood to Maturity." *The Journal of Economic History* 3 (September 1986): 721–741.

Stimpson, Jr., Eddie. *A Black Sharecropper's Recollections of the Depression*. Denton: University of North Texas Press, 1999.

Tannenbaum, Frank. *Slave and Citizen*. Boston: Beacon Press, 1946.

Taylor, Joe Gray. *Negro Slavery in Louisiana*. New York: Negro University Press, 1969.

Trexler, Harrison. *Slavery in Missouri, 1804–1865*. Baltimore: Johns Hopkins Press, 1914.

Tyler, Ron, and Lawrence R. Murphy. *The Slave Narratives in Texas* (Austin: Encino Press, 1974).

Washington, Mary Helen. *Invented Lives*. New York: Doubleday, 1987.

Weiss, Nancy. *Farewell to the Party of Lincoln*. Princeton: Princeton University Press, 1983.

Weld, Timothy Dwight. *American Slavery as It Is: Testimony of a Thousand Witnesses*. New York: Arno Press, 1968.

White, Deborah Gray. *Ar'n't I A Woman? Female Slaves in the Plantation South*. New York: Norton, 1985.

Williams, Roy, and Keven J. Shay. *Time Change: An Alternative View of the History of Dallas*. Dallas: To Be Publishing Company, 1991.

Williams, William. *Slavery and Freedom in Delaware, 1639–1865*. Wilmington, Del.: Scholarly Resources, 1996.

Yetman, Norman. "Background of the Slave Narrative Collection." *American Quarterly* 3 (Autumn 1967): 534–553.

Zamora, Emilio. *The World of the Mexican Worker in Texas*. College Station: Texas A&M Press, 1993.

Theses and Dissertations

Miliatos, Ioannis. "Some Aspects of Slavery and Slave Care in Texas." MA thesis, Texas Southern University, 1972.

Moody, Alton V. "Slavery on Louisiana Sugar Plantations." PhD diss., University of Michigan, 1923.

INDEX

Adams, Will, 31, 38, 85, 106, 114
Adams, William, 43, 55, 99, 104
Allen, Sarah, 18
Anderson, Andy, 33, 40, 99, 109
Anderson, Willis, 7
Aptheker, Herbert, 129
Armstrong, Mary, 50
Arnwine, Stearlin, 43, 71, 81, 89
Ashley, Sarah, 23, 40
Austin, Moses, 14
Austin, Stephen F., 14, 121
Babino, Agatha, 29, 69
Barker, John, 62, 71, 74, 82
Barnes, Joe, 63
Beckett, Harrison, 98
Beecher Stowe, Harriet, 128
Bennett, Lerone, 67, 81
Bess, Jack, 100, 106
Betts, Ellen, 44
Beverly, Charlotte, 84, 85
Black, Francis, 42
Blanks, Julia, 10, 54
Blassingame, John, 7, 134
Boles, John, 43, 66
Botkin, Benjamin, 12
Boyd, Harrison, 46
Boykins, Jerry, 41
Bradshaw, Gus, 47, 76
Brady, Wes, 10, 84
Branch, Jacob, 50, 55
Brim, Clara, 38, 45
Brown, Fannie, 42
Brown, Fred, 63, 74, 83
Byrd, William, 29, 78, 90

Bushnell Hart, Albert, 131
Butler, Butler, 73, 89
Cade, John, 5, 133
Campbell, Randolph, 14, 29, 54, 136
Carter, Cato, 45, 54, 69, 104
Center for American History (University of Texas at Austin), 7
Civil Rights Movement, ix, 3, 132, 134
Civil War, 3, 33, 46, 55, 62, 98–100, 104, 111, 117, 131
Clark, Anne, 70
Cole, Thomas, 23, 45, 55
Coleman, Eli, 31
Confederate States of America, 97
Cumby, Green, 34, 82
Darling, Kate, 42
Davis, Campbell, 13, 29, 84, 90
Davis, Jefferson, 96
Dies, Martin, 11
Diouf, Sylviane, 69
Douglass, Frederick, xi, 10, 20, 69, 70
DuBois, W. E. B., xi, 5, 100
Duhon, Victor, 45
Edwards, Mary Kincheon, 42
Edwards, Minerva, 83, 89
Elkins, Stanley, xi, 59, 131
Ellis, John, 63
Escott, Paul, 66, 134
Evers, Medgar, xi
Ezell, Lorenza, 78
Field Order No. 15, 101
First Texas Calvary, 99
Fogel, Robert William, 66
Foner, Philip, 134

Ford, Sarah, 34, 65, 70, 109
Forward, Millie, 43
Franklin, John Hope, 37
Freedmen's Bureau, 102
Fry, Gladys-Marie, 134, 134
Garner, John Nance, 121
Genovese, Eugene, 30, 40, 86, 134
Gibson, Priscilla, 73
Gilmore, Mattie, 46
Goodman, Andrew, 111
Grant, Austin, 40, 95
Great Depression, ix, 12
Grimke Weld, Angelina, 27
Gutman, Herbert, 62, 134
Hadden, Sally, 53
Hamilton, William, 50, 113
Hawley, Francis, 80
Hawthorne, Ann, 41
Hayes, James, 73, 100
Haywood, Felix, 11, 55
Henderson, Phoebe, 62, 74
Hill, Albert, 84
Hoard, Rosina, 112
Holland, Tom, 41, 53, 63, 78, 80, 106
Hood, Henry, 31, 90
House Un-American Activities
   Committee, 11
Houston, Sam, 13, 54
Howard, Josephine, 65, 71
Howard, Oliver O., 102
Hudson, Larry, 86
Hughes, Langston, 5
Jackson, Carter, 71
Jackson, James, 72, 83
Jackson, Maggie, 72
Jackson, Martin, 10, 19, 99
Jim Crow racism, x, xiii, 3, 49, 117, 118,
   129, 132
Johns, Thomas, 65, 71, 107
Johnson, Andrew, 101
Johnson, Charles S., 4
Johnson, Pauline, 85
Jones, Bud, 113, 116

Jones, Jesse, 121
Joyner, Charles, 134, 135
Kelly, Aunt Pinkie, 74, 82, 108
Kinchlow, Ben, 75
King, Silvia, 65
King, Jr., Martin Luther, xi
Kolchin, Peter, 61, 77, 86
Ku Klux Klan, 50, 59, 114, 131, 135
Lee, Lu, 109, 115
Lee, Robert E., 100, 118
Leggett, Walter, 9, 17
Lewis, Henry, 9, 88, 100
Lewis, Lucy, 78, 80
Lincoln, Abraham, 13, 97, 98, 101, 114
Liston, Robert, 70, 79
Little, Annie, 13
Litwack, Leon, 100, 103, 134, 136
Lomax, John, 5
Lomax, Ruby, 12
Lynch, Willie, 37, 67
Maddox, Jack, 68
Maddox, Rosa, 17, 68, 81, 116
Malcolm X, xi
Manuel, Millie, 10, 26
Martin, Joan, 86
Mathews, Louise, 72
Mathews, William, 64, 87, 105
McCoy, John, 126
McCrea, Billy, 12
McMillen, Sally, 70
Mitchell, Charly, 78
Mitchell, Peter, 106
Moore, Laura, 18
Moore, Van, 32, 63
Moses, Patsy, 9
Newspapers
   San Antonio Light, 121
   Texas State Gazette, 52
   Texas Ranger, 54, 56, 57, 58
   Houston Telegraph and Texas Ranger,
      54, 57
New Deal, xii, 4, 5, 11, 103, 118, 127,
   129, 137

Index   173

Paxton, William, 17, 40, 107
Payne, Ellen, 81, 86, 98
Perkins, Lu, 109, 113
Phillips, Daniel, 87, 104
Phillips, Ulrich B., 131
Plantations
  Brown, 72
  Bryan, 90
  Burdett, 25
  Burns, 17
  Coats, 89
  Dawson, 25
  Davis, 99
  Downs, 15
  Harper, 40
  Humbert, 79
  Kilpatrick, 80, 90
  Mann, 87
  McNeel, 78, 81
  Patton, 34
  Rimes, 79
  Timmins, 51
  Tippens, 18
Powers, Betty, 63, 79, 108
Proctor, Jenny, 54, 80
rape, 14, 28, 111, 135
Rawick, George, 12, 134
resistance
  against whites and slave owners, 50–51
  militas, 53
  runaways, 54–59
Reynolds, Mary, 18, 28, 68, 80, 90
Robinson, Marvin, 123
Roosevelt, Franklin D., xii, 3, 4, 11, 19, 116, 119, 129, 130, 137
Ross, Susan, 7, 98, 110
Row, Annie, 72, 106
Ruffin, Martin, 104
Russell, Aaron, 125
Sambo thesis, xi
Sanco, Mazique, 7
Santa Anna, General Antonio Lopez de, 55
Scales, Clarissa, 17

Scott, Hannah, 13, 26
Sells, Abram, 9, 79, 80, 82, 100
sex
  breeding, 66–68
  owners and slaves, 68, 72, 75, 130, 135
Shepard, Callie, 9, 44
Sherman, William T., 101
Showers, Marshall, 18, 59
Simpson, Ben, ix, 30
Simpson, L. H., 123
slavery
  children, 61, 67–70, 72, 78, 79, 130
  culture, 16
  history, 14–15
  interpretation, 135
  marriages, 61–64, 70
  patrols, 52, 53
  violence, 16, 25, 28, 37, 49, 51, 52, 73, 102
slave culture
  clothing, 80–81
  diet, 77–79
  housing, 80–81
  leisure activities, 82–85
  religion, 86–90
slave labor
  field slaves, 33–34, 37, 43, 45, 47, 82
  house slaves, 16, 41–44
Smalley, Laura, 79
Smith, Ashbel, 28
Southern University, 5
Stampp, Kenneth, 8, 53, 59, 69, 80, 101, 132
Steward, Shelly Edward, x
Strong, Bert, 126
Tannenbaum, Frank, 67, 103
Texas cities
  Corpus Christi, 7, 116
  Dallas, 9, 51, 73, 115, 116, 117, 119, 121
  El Paso, 7
  Galveston, 9, 64, 98
  Houston, 63, 70, 73, 113, 119, 120, 123

Jasper, 7, 12, 43
Marshall, 10, 18, 59, 98, 121
Palestine, 9
San Angelo, 7, 63
San Antonio, x, 10, 11, 26, 53, 115, 116, 121, 122, 123, 124
Texas counties
  Leon County, 80
  Jefferson County, 9, 88
Texas Slaves' Narratives Project, xii
Till, Emmitt, xi
Todd, Albert, 26, 44
Uncle Tom's Cabin, 130
Underground Railroad, 49
Valentine, James, 124

Watson, Diane, 125
Watson, Emma, 44, 45, 107
Waller, Edwin, 57
Washington, Sam Jones, 65
White, Deborah Gray, 134, 135
White, Walter, 5
Williams, Rose, 126
Wilson, Emma Countee, 19
Wilson, Lulu, 26, 33, 64, 73
Woodson, Carter G., 5
Works Progress Administration, ix, xii, 4, 12, 130
  Federal Project Number One, 4, 11
  Federal Writer's Project, 4, 5, 11, 12
Yetman, Norman, 12, 134

www.ingramcontent.com/pod-product-compliance
Lightning Source LLC
Chambersburg PA
CBHW030322080526
44584CB00012B/670